Communicate
with COURAGE

Communicate
with COURAGE

Taking Risks to Overcome the
Four Hidden Challenges

MICHELLE D. GLADIEUX

Berrett–Koehler Publishers, Inc.

Berrett-Koehler Publishers, Inc.
1333 Broadway, Suite 1000
Oakland, CA 94612-1921
Tel: (510) 817-2277
Fax: (510) 817-2278
www.bkconnection.com

ORDERING INFORMATION

Quantity sales. Special discounts are available on quantity purchases by corporations, associations, and others. For details, contact the "Special Sales Department" at the Berrett-Koehler address above.

Individual sales. Berrett-Koehler publications are available through most bookstores. They can also be ordered directly from Berrett-Koehler: Tel: (800) 929-2929; Fax: (802) 864-7626; www.bkconnection.com.

Orders for college textbook / course adoption use. Please contact Berrett-Koehler: Tel: (800) 929-2929; Fax: (802) 864-7626.

Distributed to the U.S. trade and internationally by Penguin Random House Publisher Services.

Berrett-Koehler and the BK logo are registered trademarks of Berrett-Koehler Publishers, Inc.

Printed in the United States of America

Berrett-Koehler books are printed on long-lasting acid-free paper. When it is available, we choose paper that has been manufactured by environmentally responsible processes. These may include using trees grown in sustainable forests, incorporating recycled paper, minimizing chlorine in bleaching, or recycling the energy produced at the paper mill.

Library of Congress Cataloging-in-Publication Data

Names: Gladieux, Michelle D., author.
Title: Communicate with courage : taking risks to overcome the four hidden
    challenges / Michelle D. Gladieux.
Description: First edition. | Oakland, CA : Berrett-Koehler Publishers,
    Inc., [2023] | Includes bibliographical references and index.
Identifiers: LCCN 2022014866 (print) | LCCN 2022014867 (ebook) | ISBN
    9781523003129 (paperback ; alk. paper) | ISBN 9781523003136 (pdf) | ISBN
    9781523003143 (epub) | ISBN 9781523003150 (audio)
Subjects: LCSH: Interpersonal communication—Psychological aspects. |
    Communication in organizations. | Fear.
Classification: LCC BF637.C45 G5549 2023 (print) | LCC BF637.C45 (ebook)
    | DDC 153.6—dc23/eng/20220715
LC record available at https://lccn.loc.gov/2022014866
LC ebook record available at https://lccn.loc.gov/2022014867

First Edition
28 27 26 25 24 23 22   10 9 8 7 6 5 4 3 2 1
Book design and producer: Seventeenth Street Studios
Cover designer: Susan Malikowski, DesignLeaf Studio
Cover author photo: Kelsey Martin

Communicate with Courage is dedicated to my mom, Rosemary. She was a poet, author, writing teacher, and talkative lover of learning who extended herself to others well beyond what was required. She taught a lot of people (including me) some pretty terrific *Pro Moves* of her own. I also dedicate this book to Dan, who is patient when I fail at communication.

CONTENTS

PREFACE

THERE'S A LOT TO BE SAID for figuring out a mission, a purpose to which you can align yourself. Doing so helps you prioritize your precious time on Earth. My purpose? I'm here to advocate that you start taking more smart risks as a communicator. Decades of a calling to coaching and training have shown me that summoning courage to review and revamp our messaging is a wonderful use of time.

Most nights at 7:58 p.m., you can find me doing dishes and replaying the day's conversations in my head. Sometimes, I'll think of the next day's communication. I imagine who I'll be seeing, what might be said, and what I hope to achieve from those conversations, possibly a lifted spirit or an aired grievance on either side of the table. I find the full spectrum of human communication fascinating, and your journey just as fascinating as my own. Take it from someone who's always trying to view messaging from as many angles as possible; an outside guide can really help.

This book is meant to assist in your work life as much as it was built to assist in your interactions with family and friends, immediately and well into the future. As you look at the four hidden challenges, you'll likely see yourself in one or two, or maybe in all four. This is no cause for alarm; in fact, you're in good company. If you'd like to overcome the obstacles, summon some courage to engage in the exercises that follow. Think of them as investments in yourself, in relationships you have now, and in relationships you've yet to form. You can try them more than once, building confidence as you go. Change can be scary, but you likely have an inner knowing about when it's needed. That inner knowing may have nudged you to pick up this book and hopefully is calling you to step outside your usual ways of interacting. You may surprise yourself with guts you didn't know you had once you start down this path.

It took me a while to realize I'm often knee-deep in several hidden challenges myself, sometimes all four in one day. I was likely hiding from risk for years, yearning to connect with you through this book but defining the time as "not right." I rationalized that I didn't have time, and settled for a consulting career that was "good enough" but missing two key elements. First, the opportunity to be pushed by my editors and publisher to refine these ideas and second, the ability to reach a larger audience with them. I avoided clear deadlines other than "before I'm 50," starting in my 20s—impressive procrastination, don't you think? Rather than taking a first step, I replayed a set of questions endlessly in my head: Where to start with content? How to find a publisher? I'd written articles but never a book. Would words even come when I needed them?

And then the day came when the risk to remain tight in a bud was more painful than the risk to bloom.

—ANAÏS NIN, AMERICAN WRITER

I grew tired of worrying, and ready for risk. I implored colleagues at my hometown CEO Roundtable: "Don't let me return to next month's meeting without chapter outlines." Our group advisor Dave shot me an email: *Let's have lunch. I want to hear how the book is going.* My Project Manager Tim said: *Take it one chapter at a time. I'll give you deadlines.* With each baby step, the risk in sharing the hidden challenges seemed less imposing. To write openly and honestly feels like exposing my soul and inviting rejection, but if not now, when? We're only on this planet for a short time. We can get to where we're growing when we get real about where we are. Taking risks to gain power as a communicator is often more important than what people will think or say about your messaging.

I also want to mention, as you work through these ideas and exercises—you are not alone if the idea of looking closely at your communication modus operandi makes you a little nervous. And know this: there's something waiting on the other side of courageous risk-taking for you, something good, illuminating, and life-giving. Whatever it is, it won't come fully into view until you deviate from the safe route as a communicator.

I hope you find many useful takeaways here. I hope you discover jumping-off points for conversations about communication with the people who make your world. That's what I'm about, and what my company has always been about: learning through realistic (and brave) goal-setting in communication and leadership training, executive coaching, strategic planning, and process improvement programs. Our team has embraced taking smart communication risks daily and we've seen the payoffs. We're overcoming our hidden challenges by building skills, not schemes. It feels fantastic to see hidden challenges in the rearview mirror, although sometimes they reappear in the road ahead. That's OK.

It's still progress.

Get ready to try some courageous new communication thoughts and behaviors. Doing so will prove that you can see yourself and others clearly and fully, that you want to do so, and that you understand the power of words. Let's go forward bravely with open minds and hearts and see what's waiting down the road for us on this adventure. Thank you sincerely for reading!

Michelle D. Gladieux
August 2022

INTRODUCTION

THINK OF THIS BOOK as a bravery manual that helps you turn risk into reward. It's here to help you reach your potential as a communicator. There's a world of wonder just beneath the surface of sending and receiving messages when you have a clearer view of what's been tripping you up. It's time to see what you might be missing.

Great communication is a full-body, full-mind, and full-heart effort. *Communicate with Courage* encourages you to ask yourself: "How am I perceived when I'm speaking and listening? What does my best effort look like, how does it feel? Where do I bring it to light? Who in my world gets my best tries at skillful, authentic communication? Who else might be deserving of that effort, and how so?" Courageous communication can create powerful wins for you and the people who matter most to you as you leverage risk, courage, and skill.

Let's start by defining key concepts that make up the bones of this book.

COURAGE

Courage is strength in the face of fear. It means sensing what you'll test out as a communicator might expose you to negative consequences, believing that some potential benefit (even if just to fortify your skills) is worth it. The word comes from an Old French word, *corage*, from the Latin word for "heart." Courage allows us to live larger, to experience the world beyond our comfort zone. Courage means not giving in to doubt when you feel a longing to get in the game as a communicator. It's curtailing negative self-talk, asking for feedback, owning your mistakes, expressing your feelings, addressing touchy subjects, and sharing credit. It can be called upon in innumerable ways and is one of the most thrilling gifts of being human. Its power allows us to take risks to reach our personal and professional potential despite obstacles that often show up as fear, ego, societal labels, and dysfunction in our workplaces and families.

Courage as a communicator is what you show when you apply for the job you know you may not be qualified for, risking rejection. It's there when you ask the person you're smitten with out on a date, when you stand to say a few words at a memorial service, or when you squelch gossip about someone who isn't present to defend themselves. In workplace settings, courage is on display when you give an employee a more accurate lower performance review rating with genuine, constructive feedback instead of opting for an inflated rating to avoid a challenging conversation.

Communicate with Courage in title alone probably sounds like a book about saying more. But courage isn't always about saying something. It can mean being quiet when you've got a remark teed-up for a laugh at someone else's expense. It might be declining to share an answer to allow a less-experienced person to unearth their own. Courage can be found when tempering your reaction, letting another speak before you do, or taking time to get your head around information you receive when you give others the floor. Listening requires the more verbose to stifle impulsiveness and deal with the frustration of *waiting* to speak. Evolution as a communicator comes from engagement and just as importantly in some situations, from waiting to engage.

Courage is facing the Dark Side (I see you, fellow *Star Wars* fans), addressing dysfunctional aspects of communication in yourself, your colleagues, your work environment, your family, or even in your own strengths which detract from communication when overused. When you see someone publicly change their mind, admit some bias, own a mistake, or stand up for their own or others' rights or feelings, you've seen courageous communication in play.

RISK

Communication choices have to be weighed against personal and professional costs. Ideally, potential loss should not outweigh potential reward. If you're brazen in the way you deliver your messages and lose your job, we lose your voice (questions, ideas, praise, constructive criticism) in that setting for good. For example, I don't always give each CEO the whole truth all at once when I offer advice about what they could improve as communicators. I usually want to continue to improve their organization's culture with them and retain my role as advisor. So, I try to balance directness and respect for feelings in my delivery. Courage doesn't always look like going all the way there with someone. You might need to test the waters, drop a hint, ask for an invitation to share your perspective, or think twice about how to word your message. You're still summoning courage, and you stay in the game.

THE 4 HIDDEN CHALLENGES

The hidden challenges we'll address are:

1—Hiding from Risk

2—Defining to Be Right

3—Rationalizing the Negative

4—Settling for "Good Enough"

They're so important to reaching communication potential that they each have their own chapter ahead. Hidden challenges are sometimes (for me) less fun to talk about than courage and risk, maybe because they smack of "here's another thing to do that's not going to be easy." It's sort of like getting a weird spot on your skin checked out. Is this something that is going to require additional attention? I hope not. I don't have time for this. And that's one way to look at it. A better way might be: "This is an investment in my future self—a self that deserves the benefits of brave communication." It's achieved by facing risk, recognizing there's much to learn beyond what seems the one best way. It's achieved by looking at potential payoffs rather than focusing on what can go wrong, and pushing past mediocre. That's what tackling the four challenges is all about.

If you want to address a hidden challenge, it helps to inquire within about what you feel as you unearth it. When approaching change, try to feel before you start to deal. Name the emotions that come up as you consider the hidden challenges. It's likely you'll notice there's some anxiety mixed in with your excitement about what you might gain from a new strategy. Advanced communication techniques come more easily after you've acknowledged that facing a hidden challenge brings some discomfort. Otherwise, you would have faced it already, I bet.

PRO MOVES

Keep your eyes peeled for *Pro Moves*. You'll see them sprinkled throughout the book with time-tested favorites concluding each chapter. A *Pro Move* is a communication attempt, a way to send or receive messages more deftly than the average bear. It's a good try that might flop or that you might pull off with flying colors. Either way is OK. A *Pro Move* is a communication strategy others might see as involving too much trouble or skill to undertake, so they walk on by, missing a chance to get closer to their communication potential. Making a *Pro Move* requires passion for learning and a desire to improve your life, your surroundings, or someone else's life. It often means you'll use self- and other-knowledge in the action you're taking or deciding not to take. For example, you know your preference when communicating is to do or say X, but you read a situation to call for Y, so you zig when you used to zag. Maybe you stand out, stand up, or stand down, but it's not the easy choice. What is it, then? It's the *Pro Move*.

EXERCISES

When you're out to gain new skills, reading is good but doing is better. This book contains a real-life action item, a "to-do" at the end of each chapter. The exercises reinforce the chapter's key content as they build your courage. Be patient with yourself as you work through them. Each will require you to stretch in a different way. The information you gather from the exercises will inform your future *Pro Moves* as communicator.

CHAPTER 1

Strength in Vulnerability (Saying "Nobody's Perfect," and Meaning It)

LOWER YOUR WALL

If I were to begin life again, I should want it as it were. I would only open my eyes a little more.

—JULES RENARD, FRENCH WRITER

LET'S START OUR ADVENTURES in communication by taking a brave look at what seems distasteful, painful, or threatening in interactions with others so we can see what holds us back. Fear is inherent in our hidden challenges. Maybe you're afraid to the point of freezing in some scenarios, or maybe just a little nervous and feeling butterflies in your stomach. The same emotion casts a wide net. We're going to outfox our fear by changing it into a tool. When fear shows up, we'll consider it an important alert that courage is required to move forward. Then we can muster some bravery. We can say, "Fear is here. Something challenging must be coming to light for me."

Recently I've managed to find myself with a broken elbow, torn ligaments, things like that, just working (and falling) around the house. This led me begrudgingly to physical therapy, where I luckily came under the care of Dr. Brittany Knight. She's very unassuming despite all the certifications after her name (PT, DPT, ATC, COMT, CBFE, OCS, and I'm sure more achieved and more to come). We've had lots of talks about pain. I am not particularly brave about enduring it. From her, I've learned to view pain as a messenger rather than a threat. The body speaks. When I listen, I can take the time and learn new skills and exercises to give it what it needs. The same goes for our communication. Where our work or personal relationships are off-kilter, or we feel fear, it's a signal that practice, learning, and courage are required to improve our situation.

FEAR CAN BE A FRIEND

Some days fear wins; that's just a fact. It always gets me fired up when it does. I can do better, and know that you can, too. You are your own best guide. You already have natural instinct and inner wisdom. This book will add a piece to the puzzle of you reaching your potential. It's here to help you understand overlooked parts of your communication and hone your strategy with courage and conviction.

The methods I suggest have helped lots of folks release some anxiety about communication. Some of it, not all of it, but they're flying higher as communicators after studying the concepts this book shares. Even the most resilient among us have worries tucked away that get in our way as we deal with other humans.

I'm a middle-aged white woman from a middle-class family in Indiana in the United States of America. That sounds unglamorous to some, but I love the Midwest, especially the work ethic of my homeland. I'm a trainer, coach, and lucky to be doing what I love to do: encouraging you to set a higher bar for how you communicate by embracing risk courageously. I wasn't always a risk-taking communicator. In stepping toward risk as I gained life experience (got older), I've found it makes my communication stand out. Anyone can stand out as a communicator. Consider this your invitation. It's not an exclusive club, but it is SO worth joining.

Fear bolsters obstacles like our hidden communication challenges. It's also natural and can be lifesaving. Unfortunately, it can overtake our spirit and dilute our power. It shape-shifts and seems to try with a life of its own to avoid detection.

INTRODUCING THE HIDDEN CHALLENGES

No one wants to seem weak. It's hard to say "I'm afraid that . . .," so we construct cunning little tricks to prevent the "ick" feelings we're afraid of from surfacing. This protective response creates our hidden challenges. Our tricks trick us. They can become habits before we know it. The fears that inhabit human communication can be overcome with some experimentation. I view hidden challenges as calls to take part in a competition with ourselves. They are gunking up the gears of how we project and receive information. They are definitely related, but divisible into four main categories: Hiding from Risk, Defining to Be Right, Rationalizing the Negative, and Settling for "Good Enough."

The terms we use to describe hidden challenges are not as critical as having the guts to actually face them. The fears they require us to see are often just beyond our perception until we do some self-study with an open mind.

We may fear rejection or retribution if we engage more fully as communicators. That's one of the reasons harassment in the workplace isn't always reported. The cold shoulder from other humans hurts whether you're 8 or 88. Everyone wants to be accepted, to varying degrees. We might fear failure and seek to avoid embarrassment, which inhibits risk-taking in communication. All of us hope to succeed as speakers, writers, and listeners.

We might fear change or see fear in others who want us to remain as we are, which makes it hard for them to support our growth. We all enjoy the comfort of being able to accurately predict someone's behavior. Our desire to feel comfortable is a major roadblock to growth, because the best challenges for us are never the easy options.

Good for you for picking up this book if any of the above sounds familiar. Your next step will be to invest time to complete the exercises at the end of each chapter. An investment in yourself is the best investment you'll ever make.

> *Be brave. Take risks. Nothing can substitute experience.*
> —PAULO COELHO, BRAZILIAN LYRICIST AND NOVELIST

You'll encounter your fair share of twists and turns, no matter who you communicate with, where you live, or what you do for a living. We have to summon our courage. We have to start wherever we've landed, and we can start today. We can begin in interactions with the people around us. There's no staying static; we either evolve or regress as communicators.

Courage grows in proportion to the fire in your belly to pursue a communication mission. You may find motivation in pursuing opportunities to lead (influence), or in earning respect by helping others (significance), or in embracing security that comes from education, financial independence, or your relationships. Most likely, you'll value all these rewards with varying vigor and interest as you age and change, and as circumstances change around you.

OF COURSE, ATTITUDE COUNTS

There's one trait that isn't likely to change once it crystalizes unless you self-reflect and redirect it. It's mindset. It's an either/ or choice. The scary thing is many of us don't even realize we've made a choice long ago about our mindset related to communication. You can always change your choice if you want to. It's an important one to make: is communication vital and rewarding, or is it a drag, an afterthought? Another important option, and it's yours alone: will you try to appear indomitable, or instead accept your human-ness (always a wild and changing mix of superpowers and weaknesses)?

Let's investigate our attitude about exchanging messages with others. Before you answer, consider this. Optimism powerfully influences how messages form in our brain and how they land as we deliver them. Optimism requires us to hope for the best, to be vulnerable, to expose ourselves to potential losses. As we extend ourselves, our hopes might be dashed and our hearts will sometimes break. If we have a successful outcome in mind to shoot for when we communicate (such as "we're going to win more business through this presentation"), we can get up repeatedly, visualize new possible communication outcomes and get back in the game, undeterred when things don't go our way. As you take more risks, you will gain resilience.

I believe communication is a vital tool worthy of a lifetime of study. Optimism has been my saving grace through every wrong choice and cringe-worthy personal gaffe so far. My parents Rosemary and Adrian, and older siblings Mark and Mike role-modeled humor in sorrowful times. They taught me to distinguish a real disaster from a bad day. Of course, that's what we do as kids—internalize the messages and modeling we see around us as we grow up.

If you're around kids, you're probably planting some seeds in their brains by your example in daily interactions. Kids watch closely to see what the rules are in the world of communication, and they replicate or are forced to sort out later what you demonstrate today.

Optimism will be the first *Pro Move* we address. A *Pro Move* is a best practice that requires some panache to pull off. It's not about pretending everything's coming up roses. It's realizing that since one word, one act of asking or listening, can light up the darkness, we're silly not to take the risk to try. It's about working the problem rather than being swallowed up by it. Looking at the pluses as closely as the minuses and anchoring your message to them requires courage.

IMPROVE YOUR OUTLOOK AS A COMMUNICATOR

You are free to experiment with how your worldview affects your communication. We all get stuck sometimes focusing on what's wrong rather than what could be made better. To get a more energizing outlook, meaningful steps forward might include you choosing to:

1. Notice negative self-talk, then introduce a second voice to debate the critical voice. "I tell myself X when in fact, Y is probably more accurate or also accurate."

2. Be uplifting as you engage others. When you can't pull it off, it's time to recharge. Use an idea from a self-care menu (a simple list of diverse ways you relax and enjoy life) to

show compassion for yourself. You deserve to create a self-care menu. The fun part is to keep adding to it as your needs and tastes change.

3. Develop a short personal mission statement to help you keep your head up through difficult days. Answer "What am I contributing when I communicate and how does it help those who receive my communication?" Post your answer in your line of sight. (Shout out to our clients who use this *Pro Move* by placing their mission statement where they can see it!)

4. List your successes in the past few days or weeks. Notice where you demonstrate courage to achieve something you otherwise wouldn't have. Your bravery doesn't come and go. It's there, although it may be obscured by fear. All you need to do is call on it when you'd like it to show up.

5. Send notes of encouragement to people who are struggling, others who are making progress, and sure, send a note to someone who is already standing in the sunshine, succeeding. State what you admire in their values, personality, or accomplishments. Two or three sentences are enough if you don't love to write.

It pays to try to find value in literally anything that comes your way in the full range of communication scenarios, from the most negative to the most gratifying exchanges you experience. Did you know those who consider the positive side of risks often live longer? One of many studies on the topic involving more than 70,000 people was published in the Proceedings of the National Academy of Sciences. Researchers found the most optimistic were 50% to 70% more likely to reach age 85 or older. Even if we aren't as mobile at age 85, we can hope to still have our communication chops on the ready as we engage in healthy communication to bolster our wellness.

Many hypotheses about why positive thinkers live longer correlate to sticking your neck out as a communicator: talking through stressful situations, regulating your emotions and resulting behaviors, having a network of supportive people because you've been vulnerable enough to develop meaningful relationships, believing you have some control over outcomes when you take risk. Good news: looking for the positives in risk and change is a learnable trait. Gratitude and giving back are two enjoyable ways to gain skill in this area. Nongenetic factors like our mindset have a profound effect on our life span, and our quality of life at any age.

TAKE STOCK OF WHERE YOU ARE AS A COMMUNICATOR

One of the fun things about being a communication coach is guiding clients to be brave (vulnerable) enough to take what we call The Feedback Challenge. You can take it, too.

It originated in communication skills training for the 122nd Air Force Fighter Wing, the Blacksnakes. I challenged them to find out what others did and did not appreciate about working with them by asking for some honest upward feedback. It's useful to think about welcoming others' opinions in the framework proposed by Charles and Edith Seashore with Gerald Weinberg. In their book *What Did You Say?: The Art and Science of Giving and Receiving Feedback*, feedback is information about past behavior, delivered in the present, to possibly influence future behavior.

The *Pro Move* of asking for opinions (directly, and about feelings) was outside Fighter Wing protocol. For example, higher-ranking team members don't usually ask lower-ranking airmen for their opinions in this way in military culture. They assured me they could do it, said they "eat feedback for breakfast," and off they went. I was so impressed with the depth of their results. They executed the exercise sincerely and respectfully, which brought in lots of good, honest data. One senior commander later emailed me summary notes he'd taken and an action plan he authored. It detailed how he planned to make small, doable changes to his leadership style to provide what his employees hoped to receive: more frequent updates, open discussion about career possibilities, and help with conflict resolution. Those categories come up frequently for people around the nation who have the courage to investigate how they're perceived.

Choose a few coworkers, customers, and people you know from personal life, then ask for opinions about what they like most and least about communicating with you. Emphasize to people you survey they can't get this wrong; it's purely their opinion you're after. No matter their response, keep your reply sincere and short: "Thanks, I'll think about this." Say it warmly. And mean it.

Then do the thinking you promised to do. The data you receive is a gift. Take time to process both the praise and the criticism. Enjoy the praise. Mull over the criticism, but don't beat yourself up about them. You might discover that coworkers or loved ones wish for different behaviors from you, more or less of something, likely related to how you've dedicated yourself to thinking. It's your call at this point: are there habits you're interested in changing?

In *The Art of Happiness at Work* by His Holiness the Dalai Lama and Dr. Howard Cutler, we find useful insight about why it's sometimes tough to change the habitual ways we see and interact in the world:

> When it comes down to it, many of us resist giving up our misery. As miserable as some people might be, for many there is a kind of perverse pleasure in the self-righteous indignation one feels when one is treated unfairly. We hold on to our pain, wear it like a badge, it becomes part

of us and we are reluctant to give it up. After all, at least our characteristic ways of looking at the world are familiar. Letting go of our customary responses, as destructive as they may be, may seem frightening, and often that fear abides on a deeply ingrained subconscious level.

The vulnerability to even consider making a change requires a mix of courage and optimism. Facing fear while you're holding on to hope is about as far as one can get from weak. It's the "A-HA" moment in many executive coaching programs, which you are in a way now enrolled in via this book.

You deserve applause for inviting others to be real with you. In training audiences of 50 or 500, when we offer this exercise as optional, about 10% of participants take it on. It's not for the faint of heart. It's for the lion-hearted. It helps you gain power as a communicator.

Wouldn't you respect the person doing the asking in The Feedback Challenge, be honored if they chose you, and be impressed they want to see themselves as others do? It's a pretty universal outcome, that respect you'll earn, and well-deserved. Be approachable when you ask for participants' opinions, and never punish someone for being real with you. You have to look these folks in the eye and say good morning (and mean it) the next day.

Communicating with courage can change your reputation for the better. As you become known as negatively or positively powerful, your opportunities shrink or expand. Ask yourself: "What's my reputation these days, the good and bad? How would people describe me if I'm being totally honest?" Please know that for all of us, there are legitimate answers to consider under both the "good" and "bad" categories—for every single one of us.

Thousands of people around the US have given The Feedback Challenge exercise a try, and they all should have been trying to make it safe for respondents to tell the truth. None of them who shared their results with me walked away from the exercise with only praise or only criticism. We all earn both and should receive both.

If The Feedback Challenge seems like too much work, OK, I'll offer a modification that requires less time and talking. Just sit quietly for a moment. Press "pause" on everything you have going on and analyze how you likely made the person you last communicated with feel. Did they have your full attention? Did you elevate them in some way? Were you trying to feel what they felt? Any *Pro Moves* going on with you in your communication? What do you usually make people you communicate with feel? If the answer is "nothing," think twice about whether that's really the path you want to take. These contemplations help us take stock of where we are as communicators, one yardstick to measure success in life. It's a great place to start before you dive into the rest of this book, which will offer more exercises so you can think, learn, and DO.

As you ponder your effect on others, decide which descriptors you're proud to carry and which you'd prefer to leave behind as you build your reputation. I suggest a little talk with yourself about the value of lowering your defenses as you study what others see as your weaker points. You'll likely refer to your weaker points when you help others process constructive criticism, so they feel less alone. One of our most important to-dos is to like ourselves despite the truth of criticism offered by others, and it can be a lifelong process. It's wise and rare to simply recognize this truth. I think sometimes we pretend to like ourselves, puff up our chests, but hurt inside because we are still wrestling with old fear. Or maybe that's just me.

HELP PEOPLE SEE YOU IN A BETTER LIGHT

If you want people to know that you're trying to change, tell them! As you know, humans can be lazy. Those who have to work or live with you have already put in considerable effort to figure you out. If you want them to see a different, evolved "you," publicize what you plan to change. Give us a clue to watch for it. Perhaps you'll read a book, attend a seminar, receive a performance review, or have a heart-to-heart that alerts you something in your behavior merits a longer look. You'll get excited to become a better communicator, person, boss, or coworker. Good for you! Just be aware that none of the rest of your circle got that memo. Here's your *Pro Move*: let us know what your goals are.

Like muscles, your ability to remain humble as you take risks gets stronger with use. Drop hints in conversations that you're aware you can be an obstacle sometimes (and name the way specifically, a courageous *Pro Move*, I dare you). Say that you'd like to change. Apologize when it's called for. Invite others to hold you accountable.

Come up with sneaky "tells" others can use—a throat-clearing, a hand motion, a secret phrase a friend or coworker employs to alert you to your behavior. If someone will partner with you in this strategy, it's a favor for sure. Make sure you return the favor in a thoughtful way. Your helper could let you know "I noticed you doing that thing again you said you don't want to do," or "you're not doing what you could be doing." They, the feedback-givers and hint-droppers, are courageous. They're sticking their neck out for you. Have you done the same for another person yet this week? We can pause here while you send a quick email if you'd like. Could you check on their project or let them know you saw the email and thought it was helpful?

Helper people are so cool. You can gain power to flow into new behavior in real time, thanks to them. The risk here is the *Pro Move*, too: to open up the door and let 'em in. If you don't have a helper in mind, you can help yourself by reviewing your day as it ends, thinking about which communications were most important, then recalling what you did well and would do better in hindsight. Get some rest and start again; tomorrow is a new day filled with opportunities to polish how you exchange information.

Publicizing what you plan to change is especially admirable if you possess a leadership role and decision-making authority. You can become a role model for getting real. Realness is an unforgettable and all-too-rare style. You can show the less powerful that seeing one's weaker points and accepting them as one tries to change is allowed in your friend group, family, or organization. This impression management strategy is good for everybody in the workplace, especially beneficial to the people at the top. It increases their credibility as it improves company culture.

Here's an understatement: you're going to communicate with a broad range of humans in your lifetime. A few of these relationships will be lifelong. Some interactions are brief, others include decades of co-working or co-living. In every case, you want to be heard and you want your views respected. Your interaction partners want the same from you.

Human behavior researchers estimate we make a few thousand decisions daily. Each decision influences our actions. Actions create our reputation and hopefully, lead to a legacy of which we can be proud. Like those around you, you probably invest time trying to figure people out to maximize communication outcomes, whether you realize you're doing it or not.

UNDERSTANDING PERSONALITY AS A GROWTH TOOL

A solid starting point for figuring out how to aim messages to land well is to consider personality: a complex combination of qualities and preferences. There are several robust, valid, reliable personality surveys on the market and others less comprehensive but still fun. *Pro Move*: take one soon for an eye-opening look at how others experience you and what makes you tick.

One constant in personality surveys is a map of four main social styles. We each possess a mix, with stronger abilities in one or two orientations. Humans are too richly blessed and sometimes too stressed to interact from just one orientation. I refer to these styles as driver, expressive, amiable, and analyst, terms coined by psychologist David Merrill. You may recognize yourself in a few definitions below. It's a good first step toward courageous vulnerability: acknowledging that your best abilities come with liabilities if overused.

Driver (a natural leader): confident and direct, built to achieve and succeed. Does a lot in a short amount of time. Self-motivated. Downsides: blunt, likely to prioritize tasks before relationships.

Expressive (an influencer): verbal, articulate, can talk with anyone about anything. Gifted relationship-builders. Charismatic presenters. Generally experienced as optimistic, with a positive mindset. Downsides: listening skills may be lacking, may be jealous of others who receive more attention.

Amiable (a steady team player): concerned about others, fairness, and keeping the peace. Downsides: often conflict avoidant, trying to maintain harmony when healthy debate, assertion, or confrontation is needed.

Analyst (a deep thinker): researcher, quality control specialist, accurate, does not bluff, instead puts in the work to gain subject matter expertise. Downsides: may struggle with or leave others around them struggling with their tendency towards pessimism or perfectionism.

Look at the people around you—your family, your team, and show them you value their priorities through your words and actions. You can start with "I respect that X (having choices, relationships, efficiency, fairness) is important to you . . ."

Take an educated guess at personality traits others possess before you ask for a job, promotion, raise, discount, favor, or feedback, so you can adjust your approach to incorporate the other's lens on the world. Or perhaps you want to improve communication with a special someone, or an especially difficult someone in your life. Start communicating in a style that better matches their own, and show respect for it. You might create a breakthrough if you stop hoping to change someone else's personality and instead adjust your style to complement it.

THE TEAM CHECK-IN

You can polish your powers of observation in a Team Check-In to see others more fully as you start phone, video, or in-person meetings. It fosters candid communication. People will get that you respect what's valuable to them. Its usefulness extends to for-profit, nonprofit, and military teams. I've listened as a rock band from Fort Wayne, Indiana, called The Legendary Trainhoppers kicked off a video collaboration with the Team Check-In when in-person meetings weren't possible and they still had to do what they do—create.

Team Check-In works this way: The person introducing the exercise starts with a brief, honest self-report about being in the red, yellow, or green based on recent life stuff. Then, they ask the others: are you *red, yellow, or green* coming into this meeting, and succinctly, why? Red = stressed, Yellow = a few things you're concerned about, Green = all is well.

It's not a large time investment. It's a tool to put distractions aside to be present to one another and your communication purpose. This courageous question builds trust and respect as it creates psychological safety. A Team Check-In delivers its most positive results when group members respond authentically. Give it a try and you might see your coworkers more fully as you let them see you.

To excel as a communicator, you must imagine life from perspectives other than your own. I try not to use the words "must" or "should" often. But this alternate perspective–seeking is a must. Life is a radically different experience in key ways depending upon one's personality traits and many other factors. Have the courage to care about how others perceive the world, admitting you don't know, and your most important conversations will flow more easily.

A few years ago, I taught "Internal and External Customer Communication" seminars to groups of health clinic employees. Participants were asked to name someone who, in their opinion, demonstrates very good (not perfect) service and cares about how others perceive their work. The answers are inspiring. In their words, from the prompt "Great service providers . . ."

- Are brave enough to really try to see those they serve
- Are caring, with service part of their identity
- Try for excellent communication every day, in every interaction, with everyone
- Make friends more easily because they're inclusive
- Demonstrate respect by listening well
- Demonstrate humility
- Educate others in an easy-to-approach way
- Celebrate others' success
- Do whatever is needed regardless of job description
- Talk about more than just tasks (not afraid to go deeper)

One welcome result of this training was the benchmarking that occurred. Folks chose their own goals for behavior change relating to service, looked at inspiring actions in their coworkers, and chose to replicate *Pro Moves* they saw in others' styles. The downstream effect was care taken to ensure patients received the highest forms of communication this team was capable of pulling off.

Chinese philosopher Lao Tzu said the key to growth is to introduce higher dimensions of consciousness into our awareness. If we seek to understand as often as we seek to be understood, we improve how our communication is received. The brave risk is to imagine and to learn about life from perspectives other than your own. It turns out that more people take the action you hope they will when you take the approach of a curious, humble learner.

SPEAK RESPECTFULLY TO YOURSELF

It's not all about you and them. It's about you and you, too. By the end of your life, you've had more conversations with you than anyone else. It's a smart risk to look at what's really going on with the quality of that communication. Observe your self-talk. It's like a TV in the background of your waking and sleeping life. What's on? What do you say to yourself about yourself? Do you even know?

Begin to notice the tone and words you use when you speak to you. Are you helpful or humiliating? There's a fine line between humility and humiliating. Would you speak to a friend the same way you do when you're critical of yourself? My answer to that is: I hope not, because I can be pretty harsh with me. And that means I probably need to revise some of my mental scripts. I seem to really want myself to "GET IT TOGETHER," but when I'm with a friend who's down, I can sincerely verbalize their admirable traits and accomplishments at the drop of a hat. A different lens, I suppose. We get sick of ourselves.

Can we pause here to allow you to reflect on how your self-talk sounds? What's the worst that you have to say, if anything, about you? Are any unkind words you hurl at yourself really just old recordings from unfair, or perhaps completely fair, judges you once knew? Step back from the emotional charge for a moment. Jot down a few statements you speak to yourself.

I'm proud of you for going this deep and looking this closely. What you're doing right now is an exercise in courage. For each statement, ask: Can I refute this somehow? If so, congratulations! Do exactly that. Cross any untrue negative statements off your list. This is an exercise we might diplomatically suggest to others we care about who deal with overly critical self-talk and the resulting lower self-esteem. These damning statements aren't something they (or you) have to carry any longer. And by the way, if you can't logically refute the critical voice? Also I say congratulations! You found a worthy area of focus for growth, and this book is going to help you pursue it.

CHAPTER 1 Pro Move

You don't have to keep your weaker points secret. Without oversharing, gain power to flow into new behaviors by speaking a communication goal. Tell people who might care about what you're trying to change, so you're accountable to your word as you try on new behaviors.

CHAPTER 1 Exercise

Be aware (beware) of what you say to yourself. When you're proud of yourself, what do you say? Are you perhaps missing out completely on this type of healthy internal messaging?

When you're down on yourself, what do you say? Check the validity of these statements. Are adjustments in thinking needed to get closer to the truth?

Understand Risk to Improve Your Relationships and Career

ROLL THE DICE, BUT TRY TO MAKE SURE THEY'RE LOADED

Death tweaks my ear. "Live," he says. "I am coming."

—VIRGIL, ANCIENT ROMAN POET

WE'VE GOT A LIMITED AMOUNT of time to engage in smart risks. To risk wisely, we need curiosity about how fear affects us. It exerts considerable influence on our thoughts and deeds, and so deserves our respect. It's helpful to deduce where it's coming from and why it's here when it visits. It becomes self-defeating only when we scoot over and offer fear the upper hand. Stay in the driver's seat so you can navigate beyond the safe route.

The best learning happens outside our communication comfort zone. Of course, easy to say but much tougher to actually do. If you'd like to be a smart risk manager, you'll need to cheer yourself on as you leave unfounded limiting beliefs behind to work on legitimate weaknesses. We all have "development opportunities" (the polite and mostly corporate way to say "weaknesses"). Yet, it's common for people to proclaim that no one is perfect, including themselves, as they secretly continue to strive for perfection.

RISK IS A TOOL FOR ACHIEVING POTENTIAL

Playing small as a communicator means that you're choosing not to engage to your best ability. While you need to manage risk by communicating with diplomacy, playing small doesn't really suit anyone. Our potential shines inside. There's no guarantee about how things will shake out when you find courage to listen more fully or speak more openly, but I can guarantee that you're going to feel ALIVE. Anna Jameson, the Irish writer, has a compelling way of seeing the value in just thinking about what we hope to become:

> What we truly and earnestly aspire to be, that in some sense we are. The mere aspiration, by changing the frame of mind, for the moment realizes itself.

In preparing to teach "Lifelong Change Wellness" seminars for a health insurance company (Physicians Health Plan), we asked 95 employees in a needs analysis survey what positive and negative associations they had with the word *change*, if any? Positive associations included "the possibility of newness in my future," "moving forward," "upgrading skillsets," "stop stagnation," "change is a necessity when something isn't working," "growth," "when I change a long-held belief, I feel like Dorothy in *The Wizard of Oz*—with everything suddenly in color," "fresh starts," "progress," "constant and thrilling," "more productive," "different and better results," "a good thing if we're open to the possibilities," "let go and move forward," "innovation," "evolution," "avoiding ruts and complacency," "staying relevant." One person threw in—"none." I hope someone gifts that respondent this book. I'm avoiding saying, "There's always that one person" because sometimes, it's me.

The same respondents shared answers listing negative associations. Change requires risk, which brings up: "extra time commitment," "hard to take a first step," "negative consequences if not carefully planned," "lack of support," "the unknown can be daunting," "starting over," "this could backfire," "it's scary," "if you don't see the value, you may have a negative attitude," "fear of failure," "makes me think of loss," "resistance," "a scary dark place or feeling," "dragging of the feet," and you can't disagree with the person who typed in capital letters "SOMETIMES CHANGE JUST SUCKS!" I appreciate this person who used some humor. I wonder if they'd raise their hand at the training event and claim this cheeky response. We'd have a wonderful release from laughter, maybe the best form of communication ever invented. If you're presenting and can get your meeting participants laughing, you've hit upon a *Pro Move*, as laughter increases retention of the material at hand.

For a few decades, I've offered heartfelt advice about why the safe route often leaves us feeling "less than" and wanting more, even though it's a more comfortable way to interact. As one of my colleagues put it, the safe route has a downside: you realize what you could possess that you currently don't, since you avoided risk. My colleague had been a "stay close to shore guy" most of his life, and in recent years has set sail by speaking up more often. It's thrilling to see how the rest of our team responds to his voice, now that it's in use. We respect him even more because we see in his communication he's decided to respect himself. As he asks questions and shares opinions previously kept to himself, he doesn't come across as if he's better than anyone, but rather as if he's equally valuable. Tim now uses this *Pro Move* regularly, and it's one of my favorite things in the whole world to witness. A key moment came when he decided that his old ways of communicating were no longer serving him. That moment, or moments, held magic.

It's worthwhile to consider the costs of avoiding risk when interacting. As my coworker put it so plainly, you lose out on some really nice perks if you don't take a chance sometimes. The improved pay or job title, the recognition of your good idea, the invitation to the meeting or gathering of friends, the relationship improvement, the better treatment of self and others because you advocated for them, or for yourself—these are the benefits you leave sitting on the table. Others will help themselves, and you may be left with regret.

I caught up recently with a friend on the phone after more than a year. He's been through big changes in personal and professional life at the same time, like many of us. I told him about this book's goal of helping people gain courage. I admitted it might not be up his alley since he's one of the most assertive, confident communicators I know. His response: "We all lose our mojo sometimes, like I did last year. Even the most capable communicators face fear." Humble, wise words from this world-traveling IT expert. They caused me to reflect on what one can do about it when we lose our mojo, the energy that inspires our best communication. We can rest. We can take some time to engage in what restores us, then get back in the game more refreshed and ready for the communication challenges that await.

YOUR COMMUNICATION CREATES YOUR LEGACY

If you shy away from risk, you shy away from your potential. Your legacy won't live on with as much positive impact, and what folks remember about you will lack lift that may have carried them forward. I've never stood at a memorial service and heard anyone fondly recall how the departed was great at going along to get along and managed to never make any waves.

Speaking of small talk at funerals (ugh), there's a Harley owner out there—in fact, he owned a Harley dealership in my hometown—who approached me at my nonconformist, motorcycle-loving, and life-loving big brother Mike's funeral when I was 19. Mike was seven years older than me, a 6-foot-something electrical lineman with long, black hair. He must have had a lot of friends, because the place was packed. This buddy of his stood squarely in front of me at the stuffy funeral home wearing black leather head to toe and loudly proclaimed, "Don't you worry now, little Shelly! Your brother's got his KNEES IN THE BREEZE IN HARLEY HEAVEN!" I recall he was wearing an American flag bandana on his head. People stopped talking and stared at us. I grinned. His courageous communication, deemed inappropriate by some, hit the mark with me completely. I've recalled it fondly, playing it over and over in my mind for many years. It took about 30 seconds and probably wasn't a big deal to him, but it was to me. It helped heal my broken heart.

It was equally encouraging to see many of Mike's "brothers from other mothers" in full biker regalia stuffed in the pews at the service before the funeral procession. I'd never seen folks dress that way in church before. Not interested in man-made norms, they came as they were, dressed like one of their own whom they were going to miss, stepping up as authentically *themselves* as they could possibly be—a huge plus when communicating, a

Pro Move. The procession after church was led by 52 motorcycles as counted by my parents that June morning, as well as a line of bucket trucks from the power company. I saw each biker stop near my parents to offer condolences before they rode on. This no doubt required courage—to look directly into Mom's and Dad's eyes, absorb some sorrow in that connection, and keep a stiff upper lip as bikers are wont to do. Their empathic communication required effort. Three decades later, these mental images are a salve to my soul. Their collective expression of grief and hope makes me want to be a brave communicator, too. I can reflect on their example and have my courage ready when fear gives me the alert that I'll need it.

The bikers did what came naturally, extending themselves for a fallen friend through nonverbal and verbal communication. A few minutes here and there made a tremendous difference to my family. Isn't that how it goes? You never know what positive result even a split-second communication decision might influence. The trajectory of an entire life or organization can shift because of one person's communication attempts—yours! Mike's best friend Paul called me up last year and invited me over to talk about Mike when their birthdays rolled around in April. I was so grateful. That's a generous *Pro Move* you could pull off, likely today: start a conversation about a lost loved one with someone who's missing them. It's rare. It's a gift. It costs no money, just a little time.

People remember the imprint you leave on their hearts, minds, and souls. Build a legacy that can shine forward through others. It might be that you can be counted on to listen with your full attention, to speak with your imperfect voice, or to spare a few minutes to check in, share an experience, a joke, an observation, or a good question. Your communication style will be discussed. It might be as a job candidate, for example, and your communication choices in the interview are on display. Each day, stretch enough to make a difference, and that means befriending risk. The risks you take to learn are worth it.

The same year Mike passed away, we were unfortunately facing the end of our mom's fight with cancer. I vividly recall being a junior at Purdue University driving a few hours home to see her any chance I got. I'd park and run through the below-ground parking garage to the hospital lobby to hustle into the elevator to be carried up to the 4th floor to sit once again by her side. There was nowhere else I'd rather be. Again and again, she shooed me out of her hospital room to go back to campus and learn. Decades later, I still want to argue and defy this directive. She had an advantage: I wanted to stay but didn't want to make a scene and upset her or the other patients. So back to the parking garage I went, wiping tears, fuming inside, back to school, and facing the risk we'd never meet again. The risk I took to access learning—in this case, the learning available at college—was worth it, she believed, and I suppose I see her point.

The risks are not life or death in most everyday communications, although they can feel pretty imposing sometimes. As you try out a few *Pro Moves* and pair them with the exercises that conclude each chapter of this book, you will get past fear at your own pace. At any pace, at least you're moving in the right direction—toward fear rather than away from it. There's no limit to the number of *Pro Moves* you can create and attempt.

Communication is best when it's essential, when it comes from who you uniquely are. Your best communication will never be an imitation, although you can look to others for inspiration. Your best communication will often happen when you embrace risk. Little things mean a lot. Folks who don't want to try a little harder may accuse you of making too big a deal about how you or they communicate. Don't buy it.

Communication can be a gift of giving and receiving, or it can be a weapon. Silence can be a true favor to another, as you clear your mind and hold space for thoughts they need to share. Silence can alternatively be a cruel saboteur of relationships as a signal to another they aren't worth your time or effort to come up with some words. Your motive matters, and you're wise to state it. We can't read your mind (or heart)!

ROLE MODELS ARE ALL AROUND YOU

I take joy from (and notes about) the way my friend Heather Presley-Cowen, a community development consultant, gracefully says "I receive that" when she's offered a compliment or criticism that is particularly of value to her. It strikes me as a *Pro Move* as she lets the sender know their words matter before she constructs her response. Another friend, Michele Hill, earns WWHD ("What Would Hill Do?") status in my thoughts about communication prowess. She's unfailingly professional and has a deep love of data coupled with a warm heart. When I need to summon powers of logic and be centered in interaction with clients we often serve together, I ask myself, "WWHD?" And it helps. With Hill or Heather on your project, you know you're expected to work hard and take the highest road possible in communication, great things to have associated with one's name.

My friend Jean is a model of diplomatic assertiveness. She is well-traveled, petite in stature. Polite. Elegant. I notice that people like to confide in her. She says, "A wee cup of tea can go a long way." She came to the United States from Scotland over 50 years ago to make her way in a new and at times, unwelcoming culture of the Midwest. Also, she's not taking any mess from the likes of you if you step on someone's toes. She stands up for others using a stern "I mean business" style but somehow still light touch and does it all in her lovely Scottish accent. It's a *Pro Move* to identify people in your life to emulate. Choose something they do well to try for yourself. "Acting as if" helps you try new approaches. Eventually, what you admire about their communication style integrates into your own.

My other big brother Mark is just a phone call away, demonstrating responsiveness all across the family, for many years. We're 14 years apart, which means (especially when we argue) I suspect he thinks I'm actually 14 years old. To be fair, I might be acting like I'm 14. Old family roles are tough to shrug off. Mark taught me much of what I know about negotiation. He's an "act as if" person for me. From not taking my side when I'm only seeing my side, to knowing the market value of our consulting services, to not negotiating against myself, to teaching me to ponder what the other person wants as I take the risk to ask for what I want, he's straightened out my priorities many times. I especially appreciate his guidance in conflicts that feel so big it's tough to get one's arms around them when they're happening.

I wish you were sitting next to me today so we could look one another in the eye. I'd encourage (share courage) with you. You'd hear in my voice I'm *certain* you can level up as a communicator. The seed of more impactful communication is within you and every human. We must tend to it with clear purpose, knowing why we want to improve. We can chip away at hidden challenges with *Pro Moves*, taking some pages from this book. You can also design your own *Pro Moves*, which I think you'll find fun.

You'll start to move beyond career and relationship impediments that used to trip you up. Just let the people on the safe path point over to your bumpier one, judge, or stare. Let them laugh at your clumsy communication attempts. I was a ballet dancer from a very young age. It took many off-balance tries before I could land a pirouette, additional years of preparation to stand and leap in pointe shoes, and a ton of on-stage performances before I convinced my face not to telegraph my mistakes to the audience. My face was the worst tattletale. I'm glad now that I risked looking silly, because those performing years are some of my fondest memories. Give yourself permission to look like a beginner, and your critics will matter less. Mindset most certainly matters. Choose, choose, choose. Choose it daily. You're out to control your mind, so it doesn't control you.

On this journey to becoming a better communicator, if you bring along some patience and humor and commit to try the exercises at the end of these chapters, your potential is unlimited. No one can know what you might accomplish, not even you! You'll experience baby-step successes, probably some pretty spectacular failures, and everything in between. Experimentation is where some of your best learning resides.

Our mind builds walls to protect us, but we can outsmart its overprotective nature by resolving to seek smart risk. Any new growth or resilience you develop will bring you closer to peace and joy. Your posture may change as you deservedly hold your head up higher when you speak. When your head hits the pillow at night, your rest may come easier when you know you've left it all on the court. If you're OK with your communication not always panning out the way you hope, no one and nothing can keep you down.

I hope you'll believe in your ability to polish your reputation where needed. I see evidence that it's possible in thousands of people I've come to know in my career, and also in myself. There's no better investment of hope, love, energy, or risk than in yourself. You have others around you from whom you can draw inspiration. You can even look to history and to people you don't know personally but whom you admire. Benchmark their impressive efforts. Notice what they're doing in their email, meetings, letters, voice memos, videos, articles, books, and texts, and give someone else's *Pro Move* a try, adding your own signature touch.

CHAPTER 2 Pro Move

Remind yourself you can both welcome risk (which is to say, welcome change) and fear it simultaneously. Instead of burning energy to maintain status quo, trust your ability to adapt and learn.

CHAPTER 2 Exercise

Go about life as normal this week but add one ingredient: a new risk. Say or write one thing you'd normally keep to yourself each day, with a motive of being helpful, candid, kind, and real. State your positive intention up front to increase the chances your communication will be received as intended.

This exercise changes quite a bit for those of us who find participating in communication, even tricky communication, relatively easy. If verbal fluency is your thing, say one less thing to allow another to be heard without having to jockey for position in your conversation. Either way you play it, courageously move toward what's more challenging for you. With effort and a little luck, an exercise at the end of a chapter might change how you communicate, and change your life.

CHAPTER 3

The Hunt for Hidden Challenges (The Blind Spots You Most Need to See)

FACE YOURSELF WITH HEART

There is a vitality, a life force, that is translated through you into action. And because there is only one of you in all time, this expression is unique. If you block it, it will never exist through any other medium; and be lost. It is not your business to determine how good it is, nor how it compares with other expression. It is your business to keep it yours clearly and directly, to keep the channel open.

—MARTHA GRAHAM, AMERICAN DANCER
AND CHOREOGRAPHER

GENERALLY SPEAKING, it's not a great idea to generalize about humans. When we clump people into groups for convenient analysis, we're often oversimplifying their characteristics or just plain wrong. But in some cases, sorting our challenges, worries, and other things that hold us back by commonalities is useful. I find it helpful to categorize four hidden communication challenges to help myself and others understand then overcome them.

I have some good news for you! You don't need to deviate from your preferred communication style all the time. There are plenty of occasions when your comfortable style is best for the situation at hand. The *Pro Move* is to know when to stretch toward a different style, one you're less likely to employ due to life experience and your personality. The stretching you do is called situational leadership: adapting to choose the most productive style and path as you interact with self and others.

HOW COURAGEOUS COMMUNICATION IS ACHIEVED

Courageous communication is not driven by habit or personality, and it certainly isn't driven by fear—although what makes us anxious can illuminate our opportunities. Where fear and risk-taking meet, we find courage. Courageous communication is achieved through self-knowledge, practice, and a desire to use one's gifts, such as resilience, to be better today than yesterday. It's courage that propels us to look more deeply at ourselves, at parts we perhaps haven't yet invested the time or effort to see.

I've witnessed an interesting benefit that happens as a result of coaching clients practicing new behaviors. What they try on for size in their personal life, perhaps switching up their usual family communication role, creates skills that map over to their work life. It works in reverse, too. The baby steps you take in your work life to use courage in your interactions will help you get outside your comfort zone in personal situations as well.

There are many benefits to be had from your experimentation. The late, great Tom Petty (one of my favorite artists of all time) offers a broad catalog of songs to add to your courage playlist: "I Won't Back Down," "Runnin' Down a Dream," "Only a Broken Heart," and "Even the Losers," to name just a few. More than 80 million records sold and a 40-year career of sold-out shows later (and no fear in standing up to top brass at record companies when a deal was bad for himself, his band, or his fans), wow, did this man leave a legacy as a communicator. You, too, will be working on a mystery, going wherever it leads, because the gifts that stem from communication risks are never exactly knowable. They tend to reveal themselves as time passes. They can deliver you to success in roles you might not have previously thought you could handle as others notice your commitment to doing the right thing, the brave thing, in the face of fear.

It can be tricky to suss out which challenge you most need to address. I bet you knew deep down when you saw this book's title that there's something you've been trying to ignore or outrun. For example, I can be controlling. I like to achieve my goals, which is a good thing, but when I overuse that quality, my communication takes on a bossy tone I'd rather not hear. I'm sure others would rather not hear it as well. When I ask myself, "What's driving this behavior?," my inner voice tells me I'm controlling situations in an attempt not to lose what I hold dear. Loss has happened to me (and likely to you) enough times that control feels like a pretty good strategy. Of course, it is often not, as rigidity does little to help us with change.

Your mindset and outside influences attempt to dictate how you see yourself and how you communicate with the outer world. There's a lot of feedback—some helpful, and some really not—coming at you nonstop. It's so much input, you can't possibly recognize or question all of it, and it's even harder as a solo effort. This chapter will help you see how the hidden challenge you most need to see is likely an overuse of a strength, and it will start you on a path of smart risk-taking adventure. Get on down the road so you can pick up whatever's yours!

Where to start? As it's often said, awareness is a good first step toward positive change. Until we identify and accept what's blocking us, we can't overcome the obstacle. We simply can't battle what we can't see. Read on for examples of how as a teacher and coach, I see hidden challenges manifest in people I've helped. I am not a fan of these sneaky obstacles. They really slow people down and hurt their chances for fulfilling relationships and work. I do respect them as useful learning tools. I hope you find yours, I find mine, and that we can obliterate them using *Pro Moves* and baby-step strategies. Together, let's find the right hidden challenges to understand and untangle.

IDENTIFYING WHAT YOU WANT TO CHANGE

Jazz great Miles Davis instructed us, "When you hit a wrong note, it's the next note that makes it good or bad." Identifying what to change and trying new behaviors is the crux of growing as a communicator. What Miles conveyed is essential in music and in communication: you will at times forget even your most sincere resolutions or your words won't come out right. They may not come out at all. You'll make some faux pas. It's what you do after the stumble that will set you apart from many other people: you get back up. You clarify, apologize, reword, revise, restate, recharge, retry, and inch ever closer to your communication potential because you are resilient. And you have *Pro Moves* in your pocket.

Albert Einstein's colleague John Archibald Wheeler, a physicist who communicated with him over the course of 21 years, published an essay about Einstein in *Newsweek* magazine in 1979. He noted that Einstein employed three rules of work. 1. Out of clutter, find simplicity. 2. From discord, find harmony. 3.

In the middle of difficulty lies opportunity. Number three relates well to our pursuit of hidden challenges, and how we can view them. Rather than "ugh, I have to work on myself," let's find some opportunity in the difficulty of hidden challenges, shall we?

First up, **Hiding from Risk**.

You likely know it if you do it. It's a feeling of low confidence—a hanging back, shrinking violet vibe. If I may be blunt (one of my strengths and, of course, also a weakness), Hiding can result in failing to meet life's communication challenges. One might say it results in failing to meet life itself.

Many otherwise logical people suspect they might be a "bad person," when, really, they are not different from the rest of us: a blend of good and bad. So, they don't offer as much in the way of getting to know them below surface level. I would much rather chat about their greatest regrets or most "out-there" goals than discuss what the weather's supposed to do tomorrow, but they direct communication to more mundane places, their real selves under the radar. Being seen can be scary.

Hiding causes the rest of the world to miss out on what makes them uniquely interesting and beneficial in the way they could interact. They tend to resist sincere compliments. They might allow tough previous circumstances to lead to fatalistic thinking. The mud they've trudged through thus far in life invites negative self-talk to boggle their self-view. They stop daring to stand and be counted, or perhaps have never really tried it. And this fog extends to eclipse how they perceive others' ideas. I've noticed when we're handicapped by past failures, we tend to also be quick to point to the likelihood of failure ("that's been tried, it didn't work," "it's not worth the drama to have that discussion") as a defense to avoid risk.

Just like there are no bad dogs (just bad owners), there are no completely incapable communicators. You've got some good juice. You've got a foundation to stand on, even if it's built on seeing others do or say things you never want to repeat. If we work from where we are, we can engage more bravely, authentically, and professionally with every passing day.

Hiding may come about because we're missing an important ingredient to self-esteem development: someone to say "you can do anything you set your mind to." Or, perhaps we did hear this important "you have potential" message but didn't believe the person saying it.

It is in fact quite likely you can do anything you set your mind to, from hiring and training a team, to speaking up about what makes you uncomfortable or delivering the best presentation your boss or customer has ever heard. Persistent baby steps are the way. Regardless of whether or not you had a role model to affirm your basic goodness and strengths, you can do this for yourself today. Reflect on times you've survived, times when you've thrived, and qualities you possess that allow you to keep on keeping on.

Writing about the trials of Shaker life in Pennsylvania in the late 1800s (like the conditions of public roads, the struggle to keep warm burning coal in the winter), Brother Daniel Orcutt captured a valuable, never-give-up mentality through the power of his pen:

> Do not despair at slow progress; little by little great things have come to pass. Life, and great things are made up of little things, and little things often lead to great results.

Hiding points to a fear of being exposed. If we ask for feedback (for example, about how we came across in a meeting) and something critical is said, it can trigger worries that we're not and have never been good enough. Good enough for what? Good enough for whom? How about we just aim for good enough to want to get better?

Carrying around fear of embarrassment cuts into your where-withal. It means you'll need more reassurance than others who can tolerate the feeling, and worse yet, you may fall victim to victim thinking. What a cross victim thinking is to bear! We all go there sometimes. It can feel darkly good to congratulate ourselves on our burdens and to rehash the times we've been dealt bad cards. Victim thinkers can be very strong-willed as they adopt a hiding perspective. It would be to their advantage to apply their impressive will to embrace risk rather than to avoid it completely.

Another word about victim thinking. It reinforces itself. It's exhausting but often possible to find something or someone "out to get you" in every interaction. We unlock this cage when we decide to find some modicum of power to assert, no matter how crappy the situation.

A good reason to come out of Hiding is that we can't encourage others if we haven't dusted off and exercised our own courage. Folks in Hiding are not a good choice for supervisory roles despite tenure or depth of knowledge until they overcome their "fly low" reflex. They just can't credibly motivate others to take development risks. "Do as I say, not as I do" never convinced anyone.

There's another tell of Hiding: the preference for predictable scenarios is an overused strength of steadiness and preference for routine. As we avoid attention, we deny the world our fresh perspective. That's a shame, because every person's light as a communicator is singular and will never shine forth from another. Your light is irreplaceable.

IF YOU SUSPECT YOU'RE HIDING FROM RISK

Think about what you lose: a chance to make your mark in a positive way. Think about how those around you lose the benefit of seeing you more deeply and learning from your experience. Get past fear of judgment by choosing what matters most to you. Instead of seeking to blend in, make a choice to get in the game as a communicator. Not everyone will applaud your effort to stick your neck out, but you can survive negative feedback by comparing it to your values. Collect data as you interact with others and adjust your sails as needed using sources you trust as guideposts.

The second hidden challenge is **Defining to Be Right**.

Defining is claiming absolute assurance and overlooking gray areas because we don't want them to exist. Defining can be a defense mechanism. It's something that keeps us feeling safe. It's an illusion because growth is a better bet, and it can keep us stagnant. It limits conversations and our ability to bravely include competing points of view as we consider options and navigate life.

In Defining mode, we often don't believe we could be biased, so bias seeps into our communication undetected by us, detected by others. This damages credibility. We often show impressive persistence when we believe we're right, but overuse that strength, becoming unbending in the way we impose our beliefs on situations, self, and others.

I often feel Defining to Be Right fear when I tune in to clients' frequencies in coaching sessions. Many are understandably afraid to see how their belief structure, words, or actions may limit others' opportunities, because if that's true they think, oh my gosh, am I a bad person, and how long has this been true?

In Defining mode, we are quick to judge good or bad, right or wrong, because it gives us a sense of control in this crazy world. And again, we meet our old friend fear in the second hidden challenge.

Defining downplays the importance of optimism, inclusiveness, and empathy when those three qualities can actually expand a person's communication power exponentially. Definers can come across as rigid, overusing their skill of setting boundaries, which may make them seem unapproachable. They miss out on feedback. By forgetting to include competing viewpoints, they may not be included by others seeking input in return.

Defining behaviors are hard to admit (what hidden challenge isn't?). Testing what we've been taught can make us question our upbringing. It can cast a shadow on the behaviors of our past or on our current mentors or role models. As one example, it's uncomfortable to question the fairness of a society or structure when we have perhaps succeeded within an environment that's less advantageous to others.

IF YOU SUSPECT YOU'RE DEFINING TO BE RIGHT

Know that on the twisty road of communication you're right where you're supposed to be, perfectly imperfect. Nobody wants to hang out with someone who has no weak points to work on. Be a seeker. Investigate conscious and unconscious bias so you challenge your own thinking and others' thinking when necessary. Test your assumptions instead of relying on them. Inform your mind (which controls you if you don't control it) that you will remain open to diverse views. Celebrate when you have the courage to accept your opinion, data, or hunch is wrong. Keep learning, lest you limit your growth by your rules. Not only will your communication prowess expand, but so will your understanding of the world. Change won't hit you as hard going forward.

Rationalizing the Negative is the third hidden challenge.

Rationalizing is an attempt to explain or justify behavior or attitude with plausible reasons, even if they are not completely true, useful, or appropriate. Rationalizing is related to an excellent tool: logic. It's wise to turn on cognitive processing when emotions run high. But Rationalizing can lead to risk aversion and conflict avoidance.

Highly cognitive folks fall prey to a pessimistic mindset as they seek and talk about what's going wrong or could go wrong more often than what's going well or might go well. This becomes a detriment when important tough conversations get skipped because expending the effort just doesn't seem worth it.

Rationalizing can prohibit us from "going there," from going deeper than surface talk, where trust is built, problems are aired, and sometimes problems are solved. Sticking to the facts and avoiding talk of feelings comes at an unfortunate cost. Analytical, detail-driven communication isn't the only type of communication called for in many scenarios, especially those that unlock human potential, repair a damaged relationship, or address workplace performance problems. You know change is important and that there's no escaping it. When we're Rationalizing, the negative side of change seems larger than life, and we may downplay the emotional elements of communication, missing opportunities to really engage with our partner or colleague.

Because a Rationalizer's self-talk warns them of pitfalls rather than emphasizing opportunities, they may not invest fully in relationship communication. They may shy away from disagreement and have difficulty putting their cards on the table. This means those around them are stuck guessing about how they feel, so Rationalizers are assigned negative viewpoints or a lack of caring that just isn't accurate. In Rationalizing mode, we think things we may not verbalize. We might shut down, cut off communication, or project a negative tone. Rationalizing that most debate isn't worth the energy limits our own and others' success before we even begin. When we put no faith in positive outcomes as interactions get challenging, positive outcomes become less probable.

Many folks (maybe you, too?) believe the risk of something going wrong in conversation outweighs the benefits, so they "avoid the drama" by shutting down, losing their temper, paying lip ser-vice (going along in word but not deed), or by forfeiting and losing unnecessarily to escape the conversation. The result is often a stag-nant relationship. It does not feel good, and nobody grows.

IF YOU SUSPECT YOU'RE RATIONALIZING THE NEGATIVE

Ask yourself: In recent conversations, what type of presence did you bring to the interaction? How did you leave others feeling? In your next conversation, choose a quality you *want* to bring to the interaction. Do your best to project that energy. You may need to stop cutting yourself or others off at the knees. You may be in a pattern of limiting success before you communicate by forgetting to monitor your energy.

Set aside disbelief. Success is possible even when it's not prob-able. Your self-talk will be the first type of communication you revise. Then, you'll notice your outward communication becomes more creative, productive, and attractive to others.

Settling for "Good Enough" is the fourth hidden challenge.

When we settle as communicators, we do just enough in a way that's good enough to get by. "C+" effort is what we expect from ourselves and it becomes all others can expect from us. Sometimes, we employ or accumulate "yes-people" to nod their heads and agree with us, making it convenient to avoid learn-ing what people really think. At other times, we may be feeling burned out and need to rest and recharge our batteries so we can be more fully present as communicators. Folks I've seen kick this habit need some way to be made aware of it (nice to meet you, thanks for picking up this book). They may be low on intrinsic motivation—the fire in our bellies that helps us strive—or they may need to reorder their priorities to allow themselves to show up more fully, but for fewer engagements.

IF YOU SUSPECT YOU'RE SETTLING FOR "GOOD ENOUGH"

Sometimes what we stop is just as important as what we start. You can decide to stop being content with just getting by in situations that resonate with you. You're destined for greater things in those scenarios. No one's saying you have to constantly be striving (at least, I'm not). But pushing yourself to excel sometimes is good for your mind, heart, soul, work, and relationships. So, play a little game. What if, in your next interaction, you figured out a way to give a little more effort? Here's what will likely happen. You'll put pep in someone's step and add a nice glow to how you feel about you at the same time. On the flip side, you might rile someone up but bring a problem to light diplomatically, so it can be addressed—maybe even solved. Some positive self-talk will ensue. Be careful, it can be addictive, in a good way. You might start to ask yourself, "What if I give just 1% more?" in interactions (sounds like a *Pro Move* to me, don't you agree?), then find yourself doing so. You often end up receiving much more than you give.

CHAPTER 3 Pro Move

Identify one hidden challenge to try to rise above this year. It's not a straight line of progress, so plan on moving at a reasonable pace of two steps forward and one step back. Baby steps are perfectly fine as you develop courage to take risks to grow as a communicator. Celebrate in a way that's meaningful to you when you act despite fear. Don't wait for someone else to celebrate you—reward yourself.

CHAPTER 3 Exercise

To make sure your courage isn't crowded out by what's going on in your head, release one worry about your interactions every time it comes up for the next month. Choose something you're doing your best to improve, or perhaps that you recognize is outside of your control. For one of my clients, this was worrying about her accent (not easily changeable). For another, it was putting aside worry that her face would flush when she's presenting.

Write out your worry, then for one full month starting today, notice and release it when it comes to mind. Use a mantra if you like: "I have this worry, and it does not define me or rule my behavior. I'm releasing it now." You can have the worry you're breaking up with back after one month if you want, which you won't. What a *Pro Move* to build increased tolerance for risk, as you use your limited energy more wisely.

CHAPTER 4

Hidden Challenge #1: Hiding from Risk

STEP INTO THE LIGHT

To him who is in fear, everything rustles.

—SOPHOCLES, ANCIENT GREEK PLAYWRIGHT

HIDING IS THINKING YOU might be a bad person, be wrong, or that things might not work out if you try, so you avoid facing some communications and may just plain avoid being seen.

Whether you are tired of the uphill climb, are frightened by the prospect of trying and failing, hate to see a weakness come to light, have a lot on the line, are expert at avoiding embarrassment, or tell yourself "it's not worth the time," I get it, and I am not here to judge. Instead, I bear an important message. When you take an opportunity to demonstrate courage in communication, you become a role model to others. This is true regardless of your age or station in life. It's true regardless of what's in your past or what's in your head as self-talk. The key is to welcome and moderate insecurity so you can take baby steps daily toward your mission and goals as a communicator.

When we decide to be a positive influence even in negative situations, we invest in ourselves. Since we "cannot find peace by avoiding life," as Virginia Woolf put it, we might send a survey to ask others to rate performance or product. We might convince a coworker to critique how we presented. We might get the counseling help we need to outrun a cloud hanging over us. We might enroll in an online or in-person educational opportunity. We might start to lift our voice or listen as if others' thoughts really matter to us. This is when things start to change. Shrinking violets can become tall and mighty sunflowers, as I've seen countless times with training participants, college students, and coaching clients. If they can come out of hiding to rock the room, share their feelings, deliver candid feedback gracefully, or improve a conversation, so can you.

CASE IN POINT: SUBZERO CONSTRUCTORS, INC.

It might sound weird to love a company, but there some companies and teams who will always be in my heart as examples of courageous communicators. SubZero Constructors, Inc. are industry leaders in thermal construction and industrial refrigeration, based in Southern California. About 10 years ago, we worked together to launch corporate employee performance reviews that continue to this day. They're committed to the process which is now extended to field superintendents. As SubZero continues to elevate the standard in cold storage construction, they elevate their game as performance review participants—both the reviewers and recipients of reviews.

The best leaders risk investing resources to ensure employees know where they stand in job performance and growth opportunities. They know that great feedback takes time to develop, and that it's a *Pro Move* to be courageous and kind in delivering it. So many companies act as if review meetings are a bother, or a formality to be tolerated. SubZero executives carve time away from daily duties to co-author employee evaluations that their employees, in my observation, in turn take very seriously. There's always mutual goal-setting to conclude each review. Goals are revisited year over year to ensure that personal and professional development is a given if you're on this team. Seasoned team members plan for the future together with newer team members, share their power, and share concrete examples of how each rating is formed. Those magic words ("thank you") are sincerely offered in every review as top leaders affirm, coach, and empower the people who will someday be leading the company. There's plenty in this smart risk for the top leaders, too. They make more informed decisions as they learn from employees what's going well, what could be better, and what growth opportunities need to be created. As their past president Eric Dahl said to employees this year to open the meetings, "The goal of our reviews is to improve *you*, and to improve *us* in working with you."

The review weeks are a joy to facilitate, one of the highlights of my year. Meaningful, motivating reviews, the kind that SubZero pulls off annually, are the very definition of mentorship and open communication, and the opposite of hiding.

HOW TO RECOGNIZE HIDING FROM RISK

If you have a colleague or loved one who's hiding from risk, they may seem far from unsure. In fact, they may be overly sure of themselves, putting too much stock into their assumptions, or rating others' struggles as less significant than their own. They're sometimes called "black and white thinkers"—not much room for gray, putting themselves ("I'm sure I'm right") or others ("They're not management material") in boxes, filed under a label that may or may not be correct but is always limiting.

Avoidance (otherwise known as Hiding) happens as we try to sidestep giving or receiving constructive criticism or try to disappear from disagreements. Conflict is a lot like poker. We each hold five cards, options among which we choose when we disagree. We can try any of the five options in any situation, but most of us lean heavily on just one or two styles. We would do well to expand our playing style.

Here are your poker cards. Be aware of them so you can shake things up a little, maybe try something new. There is no one best method here. The *Pro Move* is to try to use what will help the situation most. Your five options when you disagree, cited in many management textbooks including *Supervision: Concepts and Practices of Management* by Edwin Leonard and Kelly Trusty, include:

> Compete: "I win, you lose."
>
> Collaborate: "I win and you win."
>
> Compromise: "I give up something and you give up something."
>
> Avoid: "I don't want to deal with this, not now or perhaps not ever; it's not important enough, or would be better addressed at a different time."
>
> Accommodate: "I'll lose so you can win; let's do it your way."

You've seen people overuse competing: starting the debate, needing the last word, and finding apologies painful are signs of this mistake. Other folks lean so much on avoiding they aren't facing challenges that could improve their relationships. This is where we find the Hiders. They talk themselves out of bringing an issue up, saying it's not going to change anything if they do (you know, because so-and-so "never listens anyway" or "is too old to change"). They tell themselves it's not worth the effort, when really, they're just trying to avoid feeling a difficult emotion. I shared this same advice to a warm, charming, dedicated-to-people Chamber of Commerce leader who is overcoming Hiding: your board members don't have to be your friends for your work to be a success. They do, however, have to clearly understand what you're doing and what you need from them.

Those who overuse accommodating are often Hiding. They might become like doormats and get walked on, afraid to stick up for themselves or others when the situation calls for it. If that sounds familiar, embrace learning mode and try to stay in the conversation two minutes longer.

Speak your position. You are worthy. Your opinion matters. If to no one else, it must matter to you. It gets easier with practice. You might find it helpful to state your intention: "This conversation isn't easy for me, but I'm working on being more direct." Speak now or perhaps you will forever be chasing and not achieving peace of mind. I recall a story that piqued my interest as a kid. My dad served in the Army Air Corps in World War II. He once elevated a complaint to a high-ranking officer about what seemed to his platoon to be unfair assignments of kitchen patrol duty. His story caught my attention because I could hear the nerves in his voice as he recalled the interaction from all those years ago—waiting in the hallway, entering the commander's office, being asked to sit down. He explained that sometimes you embrace risk despite possible negative repercussions because it's the right thing to do.

It's common to overuse one style in conflict. I certainly do! It's also possible to incorporate more of the style you underuse when you know your options, and what a *Pro Move* that would be. It helps to name some situations in which your hidden challenges arise. Hiding can come up when we see injustice and hope someone else addresses it. It happens when it's our turn to speak and we pass, or when our turn to speak is forgotten or ignored and we don't raise our hand. Sometimes it's present in our failure to give genuine feedback. A study published by Lupoli, Jampol, and Oveis in the *Journal of Experimental Psychology* in 2017 examined the emotional roots of what's called "prosocial lying." Prosocial lying is soft-pedaling feedback to avoid hurting another's feelings but in so doing, depriving them of an opportunity to improve. Subjects were influenced to show compassion as they were told that a person whose performance they were evaluating had just suffered a serious loss. Other subjects self-identified as always having a high degree of compassion. In both cases, those folks were more likely to tell prosocial lies, avoiding the risk of giving the direct feedback needed to help the people they evaluated perform at their best. Two types of potential are harmed here: the feedback givers (not using their voice fully), and feedback recipients who are not getting the full story.

PUBLIC SPEAKING IS AN ANTIDOTE TO HIDING

Let's examine how we can risk using our voice closer to its full potential—the opposite of Hiding when others' eyes are on us. If you've ever said "I could never do that" about public speaking, prepare to eat your words. You are capable. If you're not yet comfortable, you can get there. If you're a natural, you can aim for even better results with practice. Speaking in front of an audience is the #1 fear on many psychological surveys. It's a pretty useless fear. Avoiding this risk "protects" you mostly from communicating your valuable, original perspective for your own and others' benefit.

Accept the fact that no presentation—even for professional speakers—goes exactly as hoped and planned. Presentation prowess is learned. I've become better at it, but as a child I hid behind my parents' legs when grown-ups spoke to me. Maybe you felt this way, too? Everyone seemed so big. They used my name; I didn't know theirs. I was grateful when the talk resumed among the adults and I was off the hook.

Later in grade school, I became very interested in science, found that I could talk to science fair judges without anything awful happening, started climbing up altar steps to read at church, and raised my hand more often in class. In high school, I ran for business club president against a popular football boy and remarkably, I won. I wasn't popular, he had me beat there. It was my messaging, which benefitted from an inner decision to stop hiding. It helped that my mom initiated a kitchen table talk about a Henry Ford quote: "Whether you believe you can do a thing or not, you are right." She encouraged me to choose. I chose to believe I could succeed in my run for that high school leadership role. It worked out in my favor that time, but either way, the choice to align with self-esteem was the real win. These days, I travel near and far to speak to diverse audiences. I can confirm that public speaking is a skill anyone can hone.

To get the most out of this risk, seek opportunities to speak in many settings. It's like swimming—any body of water will do, and each brings irreplaceable learning. Take a speaking class at a community college. Join a networking group. Go to work as usual, but going forward, make sure you participate at least once verbally in each meeting you attend. Ask for feedback every single time you present to understand how others experience your delivery. You don't have to change your style to accommodate every request. Choose and use a few suggestions as you collect reviews.

Fun fact: 100% of presenters get nervous sometimes. Risk is going to announce itself to you one of these days just as you step up to the mic or raise your hand to speak. Use risk's adrenaline as an edge. Let it rev up your passion for your topic. The audience will detect your commitment to the message and lean in. Something that helps me relax is a belief that no human is more valuable than any other. I'm no better than anyone else, so I don't speak as if I am. I'm no less important, either, so I will usually seize an opportunity to be heard.

If you don't yet fully believe you're equally valuable in this world, finding your voice through public speaking is a great way to build self-esteem. Remind yourself, this meeting, this training, speech, or toast—it's not about you. It's about your audience and your content. You are in service to both, a delivery system. Manage first impressions intelligently by looking sharp and sounding confident. Do your homework so you're closer to expert in your topic. There's no harm to admitting you're learning, or that you need to research a question when you don't have an answer. Ask for live input if you're presenting to an audience already educated about your topic.

Research in this risk-taking arena reveals your listeners are paying attention mostly to your body language. Is it awake, relaxed, and engaged? Second, listeners tune in to your voice. Is it audible but never monotone? Just as most of us have to work to accept various parts of our body, we need to learn to accept our voice, which is part of our body. Less intensely than tracking your body language and voice, listeners will track your words. This means that even if you trip over them, you can't lose with an audience if you're projecting "I want to be here." What a great reason to keep confessions of nervousness to yourself (or share those with a good friend, but not your audience), a *Pro Move*.

Speaking of audiences, check out the end of this chapter for an exercise many presenters like myself have found to be worth its weight in gold. It's called an "audience analysis," and it's useful whether you're addressing one person or many.

PRESENTATION POINTERS

A few *Pro Moves* as you call upon your courage to speak more often:

- Succinct stories that illicit emotional response are great hooks.
- Vary your voice to capture attention: modulate volume, rate, pitch, pace, and tone.
- Comparisons and analogies are powerful. What does what you're explaining remind you of? Help us see, smell, or sense what you're describing.
- Repetition builds retention. State your most important point more than once.
- Move while you present. Make eye contact, a true show of courage. It's a vital connection. If you don't meet our gaze, we're not likely to believe you.
- Pause occasionally to let all that great stuff you just said sink in.
- Start a "spice file" to add some zip to your messaging. Stockpile notes, pictures, and quotes for future communications and presentations.
- Ask others about what you did well and could have done better after you speak.

In any audience anywhere, most participants root for you as you speak. If you want to be there, we can tell. If you don't, we feel vicarious pain. We want to enjoy your speaking success because it feels like we succeed right along with you. We want to know the point of you speaking with us, as Joel Schwartzberg puts it in his 2017 book *Get to the Point!: Sharpen Your Message and Make Your Words Matter*: "Once a presenter has a point, the next most important job is to effectively deliver it. If the point is received, the presenter succeeds. If the point is not received, the presenter fails—regardless of any other impression made." Enjoy this opportunity to make a point. It's not a life-or-death risk, and you will survive the nerves. You'll get better at delivering your main point (and less anxious) with every attempt. I visualize the day when there's a real or virtual room full of people eager to hear what you have to say before you even start. Are you doing the same?

CHAPTER 4 Pro Move

Let us see you a little more fully. Let those you trust tell you how they see you. As you take these communication risks, you quiet your inner critic and step away from Hiding as a coping mechanism. Unkind or unprofessional outer critics matter less. You'll be too engaged in learning to let the turkeys get you down.

CHAPTER 4 Exercise

It's always exciting when you embrace the courage it takes to stop Hiding and get on the mic, so to speak. Seek opportunities to speak. Before small- or large-scale public speaking, do an "audience analysis" for rock-solid presentation prep, always a *Pro Move*.

- What job titles and skills are represented in your audience?
- How much knowledge of your topic do they have? What else do you have in common?

- What is their attitude toward your topic and toward attending the presentation?
- What constraints do you face with this audience or setting?
- What do they hope to get from you? What do you hope they'll do with your message?

CHAPTER 5

Hidden Challenge #2: Defining to Be Right

GET A BROADER VIEW

Luke, you're going to find that many of the truths we cling to depend greatly on our own point of view.

—OBI-WAN KENOBI, JEDI MASTER

COMMUNICATE WITH COURAGE was built to help you win. To possess effective communication skills, we need to face the fact that when we act on bias, we lose. We might enjoy some comfort if we move through life with blinders on, but we lose in the long run if we consider one human more valuable than another.

Defining is thinking you have all the best answers or the only answer. You might think bias doesn't influence your communication when it does for all to some degree, consciously and unconsciously. Not only might those people we stereotype or think of as inferior miss out on opportunities because of our bias, but we miss out on good stuff, too. There's a mountain of research pointing to the advantage diverse viewpoints can bring. Less head-nodding and "I think so, too" (which can devolve into group-think), and more "I see it differently" helps with problem-solving. Diverse experiences of heterogenous humans add creativity and innovation to any kind of process.

DEFINING COMES AT A COST

Similar-to-me effect has created many homogenous teams in organizations today. It's often easier for us to communicate or associate with those who most resemble us. It takes more time and effort to work around differences. Intentionally extending ourselves outside our comfort zone pays off when we seek diverse thought and build diverse teams.

We lose brainpower in organizations when we don't practice inclusive hiring and promotion decisions. These types of decisions are too often based on job-irrelevant characteristics (age, race, gender, sexual orientation, etc.), which precludes diverse thought and discussion. When human differences are present, we are challenged to think outside our usual perspective. This helps us avoid Defining, so we don't end up with simplistic and often inaccurate views of the world around us.

Defining from a singular point of view means we lose the chance to role-model fairness. If you're in a position of power such as a supervisory role, you might confidently state your opinion (unaware of blinders you may be wearing) and pass bias on to others. With that limited view, employees can make shortsighted choices, or may have other ideas you never get to hear. You have another option available that will grow your courage. Invite dissent, invite constructive criticism, invite other viewpoints, and then praise those with less positional or personal power when they engage. It's a good bet that when you demonstrate your interest in fair consideration of other views, you'll get more of them.

We teach "Smart Selection: Best Practices for Interviewing and Hiring" courses around the US. It's clear that Defining creeps into these types of decisions. Let's look at how Defining affects many hiring managers' choices about who gets a job offer and who doesn't. It shows up in various ways, including:

The Law of Social Similarity—We tend to prefer and choose people we perceive to be like us. Let's say the interview is live and hosted by an employer, not happening via video. I coach job candidates to take a quick look around the hiring manager's workspace and note any personal effects displayed to which they might have a personal connection. ("Looks like you have kids the same age as mine!" or "I see we're both—fill in the sports team or alma mater—fans!") It's a conversation starter that plays on this Law, and the astute hiring manager will do their best to forget the job-irrelevant parts of the meeting.

Halo/Horns Effect—This happens when we allow one positive or negative trait to influence how we perceive the person as a whole. If you seek to hire a receptionist and the last one was frequently late, your first question might be about punctuality. If the job candidate shows you attendance awards and insists they prefer to be 15 minutes early to work, you may not see where they fall short of other job-relevant skills, because you're just too darn excited that you've found someone who's reliably on time. That's Halo Effect.

Too much talking, not enough listening—Some interviewers talk more about themselves than they do the candidate. I love an interviewer who shares a few of their unique experiences in the organization, especially what they enjoy most and what real problems exist, but the main goal is to ask open-ended questions. These expose the candidate's best strengths and development areas so you can make an informed decision.

Stereotyping—This cousin to Defining is a shortcut used to avoid thinking about people more fully. It introduces bias to interaction and means you're judging a book by its cover rather than its contents.

Order of interviews—Earlier candidates may have an advantage if the interviewer becomes tired of interviews. Later candidates can be more easily memorable.

Inconsistent questioning—To build in fairness, use an interview question outline. Keep root questions the same for all candidates. Deviate from root questions to follow candidate answers about their strengths and weaknesses, making sure you can offer proof that your questions are job relevant. This keeps you from veering into Halo and Horns Effect territory.

Another *Pro Move*: take the risk to admit to yourself you're not as objective as you want to be. That alone helps you be fairer when comparing candidates.

When you speak or act on bias, people notice. They trust and respect you less. To the more fair-minded and forward-thinking, you can be seen as behind the times at best, unethical or to-be-avoided at worst. Definitely not a *Pro Move*.

As a consultant, I'm always visiting organizations, but usually not staying long. I appreciate it when people take me aside to offer insight into their culture or group. One day, I received a warning about a team I was heading in to teach: "Have fun with that, Michelle, they're all Millennials!" The communicator winked, assuming I'd know and insert the commonly held age bias that follows this age group around. The same day on a break from the seminar with the team of younger folks, one of the participants asked if I'd offer their boss some coaching, then cautioned me that this person was "likely too old to change."

Man. It's everywhere, this Defining trait. It's in me and it's in you. As with every hidden challenge, it's present in all of us, and that's not always a bad thing. But we keep our brains younger longer when we test our assumptions and really make our minds work. Many of our assumptions may not be based in fact. This requires risk: to change your old belief system and build a new one. If you do, others may be watching and learning from you.

Treating humans as equally valuable at their core offers all kinds of benefits. Social and emotional perks come from turning your attention to inclusion, to name just two. Striving to be inclusive improves communication literally anywhere you go. We've done hundreds of "climate surveys" in American organizations since the year 2000. Guess what comes up in every single survey thus far as the #1 most-needed improvement area on teams? You guessed it. Communication.

Even if we weren't raised to embrace diversity, we can begin to recognize biased thought. It's the foundation for discriminatory words and actions. Monitoring what we're thinking can prevent us from acting on bias. We become more inclusive. We can become the person who takes action when they notice someone being left out. We become the kind of courageous, risk-taking communicator people look up to. We become less easily replaceable on our team.

REDUCING BIAS IN OUR INTERACTIONS

A few key points about bias are worth your time to consider, so you're aware where you may fall into the trap of Defining:

- We all have biases. Its negative effects are lessened if we seek to appreciate differences in beliefs, choices, interests, and culture. We can admit to ourselves that we continue to harbor bias if we don't confront our mental scripts about traits we may assign to others unfairly— often, before we even come to know them.

o We all witness harassing acts and unethical discrimination in our lives.

o Since the passage of the Civil Rights Act in 1964, it has been illegal in the United States to allow adverse employment actions based on color, sex, religion, and nationality. Despite additional legislation passed in 1991 designed to strengthen the law, our nation still struggles to uphold it.

o Harassment prevents teams from reaching their full potential. It shows up in verbal, visual, physical, and silent forms. Federal agencies like the Equal Employment Opportunity Commission receive around 12,000 charges of bias and discrimination annually in the US. Approximately 80% from women seeking fair treatment at work, 20% from men, and harassment cost employers millions of dollars annually.

o You build a good name speaking up for what's right or against what's unfair. It especially takes guts to speak truth to power.

o You have a right to raise the issue of bias in the workplace under Title VII, which prevents an employer from discriminating in any term, condition, or privilege of employment based on job-irrelevant characteristics.

o We benefit from developing empathy for those we perceive as different. Open-ended questions asked respectfully are a great place to start. Check out the exercise that concludes this chapter for some conversation starters.

o Humans can work toward common goals even as
we experience the tension of diverse opinions and
backgrounds. Conflict is a tremendous growth tool if
you do it right.

My company had the pleasure of working with several hundred police officers to teach harassment and bias prevention seminars. We gave equal time to instruction in stress management strategies in a two-hour seminar that ran long each of the 14 days of training, thanks to lively, productive discussions.

I demonstrated one of my biases when every day, driving to training, I'd see one of the many police officers on their way, too, behind me on the road. Cynical from past interactions (largely, when I was at fault for speeding), I completely forgot that this learner was my customer. I'd think (or say aloud) something negative about having a police car behind me as I drove to the event. I was stereotyping the people I was supposed to be teaching to avoid stereotyping. It drew some laughter when I confessed my bias during class. Many who judge law enforcement do so without remembering that the profession is much like any other. Some amazing, ethical, mission-driven individuals work within it, and there's also a percentage of the population who are not deserving of the power vested in them.

Our training experience with these clients included spending time riding along with patrol officers, observing confinement officers interacting with inmates at the jail, interviewing detectives who give up peace of mind (as do many on this team) to attempt to solve or stop crimes. To sum it up, we had our eyes opened to a line of work I previously had formed opinions about from TV shows and limited actual interactions. We learned about the culture of their department—a must if training was going to hit the mark and stick to change behaviors. We facilitated discussions with those who hold the power to resist Defining, officers who can model inclusivity, including:

- Focus on others' behaviors and challenging one's own. For example, who do we ordinarily pass up when sharing information and who could we include going forward?
- Learn from people who've been the target of bias, whatever they're willing to share.
- Plan responses that are useful when we encounter bias ("I don't think you meant it this way, but . . . " or "Let's say X rather than Y. X can be inaccurate and offensive.")
- Promote ideas from diverse sources, not just "similar-to-me" or powerful sources.

We stand to gain knowledge—so useful in *Pro Moves* later—when we include overlooked people and viewpoints. We all stand to lose personally, as organizations, and as a planet when we don't. We need all the perspectives and voices we can get to tackle problems we face as a species, that is for sure.

Useful self-study questions so you don't jump to Defining include:

- Does this person remind me of anyone in a positive or negative sense? (They are not that person.)
- How do I feel about their characteristics such as gender, appearance, age, ethnicity? (These aren't job-relevant traits, but knowledge, skill, and ability are.)
- What assumptions do I make about their home region? (It's not a fair yardstick.)
- What do others want me to think about this person? (Run the other way when someone tries to tell you what to think of someone else.)

- How do I usually react to this "kind" of person? (The question alone reveals bias.)
- How do my responsibilities affect my tone and behavior? (Have you "defined" yourself as the only person really working hard?)

USING POWER ETHICALLY

As you gain and use power, it's to your advantage to become known for ethical use of it. Be a person of your word. Let your deeds show your thinking process doesn't intentionally leave out others who are not like you. Power is invisible, often it's there for the taking. I say go for it. We need more ethical people interested in gaining power to improve their workplaces and communities. Is it ethical to want to be more powerful? I think so. It's a *Pro Move* to strategize about gaining influence so you can make an impactful difference in your interactions.

Some tactics that work and are worth the risk when used sincerely include: showing gratitude, getting to know people with decision-making authority, getting to know people who think/behave/believe differently than you, being a broker of vital information by staying informed in your area of expertise, partnering with experts, making a positive, fast showing on tasks, returning favors, and being early to accept reasonable changes.

Moves that often relate to Defining and cross a line to stray into the unethical power tactics include: sarcasm or "joking" delivered to damage another, speaking poorly of others when they can't defend their reputation, starting infighting with a goal to divide and conquer, playing territory games, failing to report or address unethical behavior, creating false crises, or misrepresenting one's ability, intentions, or knowledge. The results of these behaviors are wasted time, damaged trust, lower morale, and higher turnover in an organization. Personally, they'll tank your reputation, something you can't afford to risk.

Leaders can summon the courage to communicate about acceptable vs. unacceptable behaviors by diplomatically stating what they see in the behaviors of those they lead. Keeping an eye on our self-talk helps limit Defining. It's a dangerous assumption to summarily define ourselves, our families, companies, or teams as "unbiased." It's likely untrue, and it's costly as communicators because we lose vigilance and courage. We'll need both to call out unethical or exclusionary communication behaviors that will likely appear and require confrontation from time to time.

CHAPTER 5 Pro Move

When you act on bias even unconsciously, you lose credibility, trust, opportunities, ideas, and respect. As a remedy, focus on building empathy. Empathy is intellectual identification with or vicariously experiencing of feelings or thoughts of another person. Our world is in dire need of more empathy in everyday communications. The best way to build it is to press pause on your self-focus and consider joys or tribulations another might be facing. Whether you're watching a news program about strangers or listening to a friend's troubles, try to feel what they're feeling. You'll be able to be there for others in a deeper, more useful way as you expand your ability to connect. The next exercise will help you to rather casually conduct an informational interview to build your ability to feel and summon empathy for others.

CHAPTER 5 Exercise

Ask a few open-ended questions to someone you perceive as different from you to learn about how they experience something you have likely not experienced in the same way. This exercise requires courage to admit that you've got a limited perspective on many things in life. Do some research on your own first, seeking out writers, speakers, or webinar/video presenters with direct experience in the area of interest. Get a little background so you're starting at a more informed place. Then make a humble approach to speak personally to someone more experienced in that topic. State your motive (to learn) so your questioning is less likely to create defensiveness. Don't assume you'll get a "yes, I'll talk to you about this," because no one owes you their time or explanations. Any personal experience they're willing to share is a gift that can widen your perspective. Both parties who agree to this exercise are demonstrating rare courage to take risks as communicators. Here are a few conversation starters:

- I have limited perspective on X and would like to learn more.
- Would you be willing to share some thoughts about this?
- What about this subject is important to you?
- What might I not know about X that I should learn?

CHAPTER 6

Hidden Challenge #3: Rationalizing the Negative

PESSIMISM DOESN'T PAY

> *People have a hard time letting go of their suffering. Out of a fear of the unknown, they prefer suffering that is familiar.*
>
> —THICH NHÂT HẠNH, VIETNAMESE MONK
> AND ACTIVIST

RATIONALIZING CAN LOOK like using logic to sideline risk as you shield yourself from the trials and benefits of engaging in conflict and other challenging communication. One of the best ways to find courage to attack fear was offered to me in simple terms by one of the most savvy and generous communicators I've met, my friend Surge. We met in college at Purdue in West Lafayette, Indiana. We had many late-night phone conversations and weeknight dinners about the various slings and arrows of that time in our lives. Whenever I was at the end of my rope, he'd encourage me (and others he cares about) to "Work the problem!" rather than to ever give in to feelings of despair. At one particularly sorrowful junction in my life postcollege, I remember his empathy oozing through the phone with him still pointing to something to be grateful for: "Michelle, to feel this pain is also to know you're fully alive."

You've probably shared courage with more people than you know if you've ever listened to a friend and tried to feel what they're feeling. It's no secret that emotional conversations can be painful. When you mix in opposing sides it can be even more painful. Yet we need to think and talk about disagreeing and its importance in our lives. We need to engage in the difficult-to-discuss stuff with more skill derived from practice and less fear. Everyone needs to know how to disagree productively, so we can aspire to bridge gaps between differing belief systems.

CONFLICT IS WHERE MOST GROWTH OCCURS

The study of conflict was one of my first true loves. A preschool teacher sent a note home to my parents in the 1970s. It said, "Today, Michelle observed a schoolmate misbehaving and suggested we take a different approach with the child." I had to laugh when this hint about what I'd end up doing for a living turned up in a musty box from the back of a closet. As a young teacher, I was hooked on any research I could find about negotiation. I remain eager to teach conflict management at every opportunity.

As a graduate school project, I designed negotiation training for manufacturing supervisors. The challenge was to get them to care what a 22-year-old had to say about the subject. It worked, thanks to a few great professors and people who invested personal time mentoring me as I prepared to teach. Dr. Jill Ihsanullah built my confidence by repeatedly encouraging me that this risky challenge was worth undertaking. She offered unfailingly wise framing of the communication challenges and accompanying emotions she knew likely lie ahead. I walked into that manufacturing plant prepared to face some tough judges of my presentation's usefulness confident despite my nerves. It has brightened my life to teach others some of what Jill has taught me. It's underscored the importance of seeking mentors who have traveled similar roads to those we embark upon as communicators whenever possible.

In the past few years, my team's training reach has grown. Participants from many states and backgrounds want to gain skill in managing disagreements. Here's what we tell them: conflict skills are never set in stone. They can improve with attention and effort. We guarantee this to those who take risks in the name of learning better ways. We coach them to ask for feedback about how they come across especially in stressful communication scenarios. We ask them to study their personality strengths and weaknesses. They choose goals to hold themselves accountable, and we do our best to offer a hand up.

I want to give you an idea of the type of goals folks are choosing. This is a benchmarking opportunity—feel free to adopt any of these as your own. None are easy, and all are worthwhile. In their own words, training participants seek to:

- Leave "you always" and "you never" out of their speech.
- Ask others for changes in behavior, not changes in their often long-held beliefs.
- Share with others not only what's wrong when in conflict, but what's right or useful.
- Point out areas of agreement.

- Allow the other person to finish their sentence before speaking.
- Focus on the present and future; don't get stuck on past disagreements.

When training day comes, we remind participants they'll get out of the experience what they put into it. RISK and ye shall be rewarded. Ask your questions. Disagree diplomatically. Test theories in your real life. Invite feedback. Some are ready, and they do these things in front of their peers despite some fear. Conversely, some sit on the fence throughout the training. We hope in that case for the best: that we're planting seeds so they will later act despite fear.

Much of how we approach conflict as adults is shaped, for better and worse, by disagreements we see growing up. The ways we engage in challenging conversations affect self-esteem—our own and others'. Our debate style affects how people behave toward us and is even more critical if we have authority, because conflict left unattended or poorly attended creates havoc on teams and in families.

I hope you'll refer to this chapter when you've got a disagreement or emotional conversation on your hands. You can consider new ways of approaching it—in other words, you can try some *Pro Moves*. You'll be in learning mode. Invigorating! And you can do so with less worry when you prioritize the relationship or the positive outcome that's possible. To call forth courage, I often think of how aviation pioneer Amelia Earhart framed it: "Decide whether or not the goal is worth the risks involved. If it is, stop worrying."

OUR DIFFERENCES UNLOCK LEARNING

To better cope with tricky conversations, look at the roots of tension, what causes it. Competing goals or lack of clear leadership creates division on teams. Changes in the way we use time, money, or space start disagreements. Walls can form around various parts of an organization, team, or family.

As workplaces become more diverse, there's a lot to disagree about if one doesn't try to understand opposing viewpoints. You may differ in age, personality, ethnicity, gender, physical abilities, sexual orientation, work background, income, marital status, spiritual beliefs, geographic location, socioeconomic status, family structure, or educational background (whew, and even more) from people you partner with to achieve goals. This will be less likely if you're in a geographic area with less diversity or if your organization hasn't successfully reached out to diverse groups. You may find yourself in a position to speak truth to power about lack of diversity in a group to which you belong, and can call upon courage to take that risk.

Differences make us stronger as a species, but biological and cultural diversity can limit our ability to understand one another. Left unaddressed perhaps because someone rationalized it as not important or addressed clumsily or with ill intention, conflict becomes a damaging force.

Parker Palmer is an author and activist who has lived through many polarizing periods in US history. He writes about human differences in a way that speaks to me. I hope it will speak to you. We share this quote from his book *Healing the Heart of Democracy: The Courage to Create a Politics Worthy of the Human Spirit* often in harassment prevention seminars:

> We engage in creative tension-holding every day of our lives, seeking common ground. We do it with our partners, our children, and our friends as we work to keep relationships healthy. We do it in the workplace as we solve problems. We've been doing it for ages in every academic field from the humanities to the sciences. Human beings have a well-demonstrated capacity to hold the tension of

differences in ways that lead to creative advances. Creative tension-holding is what made the American experiment possible in the first place.

America's founders—despite the bigotry that limited their conception of who "We the People" were—had the genius to establish the first form of government in which conflict and tension were understood not as the enemies of a good social order but as the engines of a better social order.

To squeeze the benefits out of tensions with others, know the two types of conflict—constructive and destructive. Constructive disagreement is called "substantive" because it's interest-based. There's a healthy energy around it. Parties discuss instead of defend positions. They try not to personalize the issue, so they can avoid being offended. They get creative with possible solutions. When both parties are heard and both get some of what they want, the relationship gets stronger. Substantive conflict is good for us and should not be rationalized away. It can be welcomed in our lives.

The other type of conflict is destructive and can involve deliberately wishing pain upon another or engaging in unintentionally harmful behavior. This type is called "personalized." It's position-based, often present when one party is giving up no ground. It can look like trying to wear the other person down with threats, silent treatment, nagging, or other detrimental tactics. If a solution is found, it's often because one person concedes under pressure. The relationship is damaged as vendettas are created. In unintentionally harmful personalized conflict (such as one coworker offending another while not realizing it) there's often room for the courageous people to bring dysfunctional behavior to light, so it can stop.

Substantive conflict, the good kind, is about a recognized issue. It starts with you, risk-taker. You'll need to succinctly state the challenge to confirm that a problem has been identified. Then get communication flowing:

1. Invite the other person to talk at a time that works for them. Set a date.

2. Keep your beef with this person as confidential as possible, so you can honestly say you're bringing the issue to them first.

3. Give your undivided attention to this discussion.

4. Like them or not, it doesn't matter. Thank them for their time and state that you believe you can get to a better place through conversation.

5. Invite them to speak first after you mutually identify the issue. Say, "Please tell me how you see X." Speak your respect for some part of their position ("You make a fair point that . . .") and check to see if you heard them right: "So your main concern is . . .?"

6. Take your turn to speak because you deserve to be heard in equal measure.

The goal is not to make disagreement disappear, although it might do just that if you uncover information that contradicts assumptions. One or both of you may say "I had incorrect information" and change your mind. This takes a level of maturity that's learned over time. The goal is to generate new energy, to move the conflict from "me vs. you" to "us vs. this problem."

I acknowledge that all of this is more easily said than done! You know you've arrived at higher ground when you feel it. It's a relief. It's a metamorphosis. Destructive emotional states evolve to constructive states through mutual problem-solving if you can get the other person to talk. You'll need to motivate yourself to initiate the discussion. Why you? Because you're the one with the *Pro Moves!*

After workplace mediation meetings, I might offer both parties a less-than-one-page agreement to sign. "Going forward, Person/Team A will start or stop doing X. Person/Team B will start/stop doing Y." We meet again in a few weeks to ensure that both hold up their end of the deal. This simple documentation is a good way to avoid regressing to less helpful behaviors.

SELECTING WORTHWHILE DISAGREEMENTS

Here's a question I get a lot: How do you know if a disagreement is worth having?

Good question. First, become aware. What are you doing or not doing that contributes to the problem or is viewed as annoying? What is the other person doing or not doing? Describe the situation to yourself as factually and fairly as you can. You may want to put these behaviors on paper. Then, think about the importance of what you observe. If left unattended, could this disagreement be damaging? The *Pro Move* is to ask yourself whether the issue affects your own or the other's reputation negatively. If so, you should address it.

Another test you can apply is whether or not the behavior affects the team negatively. If yes, it's worth a conversation. Finally, does it affect external customers or people outside your family or friend group? If so, have a chat. These three simple questions help you know when to engage and when to wait. Recall what Lebanese poet Kahlil Gibran taught: rest in reason. But when it's time to call on your courage, move in passion.

Think about your wants. What is your desired state? What do you want this person to do differently? What might they want you to do differently? You can't tell someone how to feel or what to think, but you can ask for behavior change, and vice versa.

People are more willing and able to change if you raise their awareness about the impact of their actions. The *Pro Move* is to do that before you ask for any changes. Tone matters. Aim to maintain directness and blend it with diplomacy. Show interest in the other's opinion. As you raise your game to avoid rationalizing at the wrong time, the easier life becomes and the more successful you can be.

Conflict should never be only about speaking your position. Listen carefully to the person to whom you've given your opinion, with your emotions and ego in check. It's not easy, but it's necessary if you want your views respected in return. Breathing exercises can help, and they can be done with only you in the know about how you're staying cool.

I enjoy thinking about my conflicts and those faced by people I care about. At our company, we study the angles of disagreements daily. We meet very few people who share our curiosity. Conflict sure gets a bad rap. Mention it and walls go up. It's feared due to the messy emotions it unearths. Despite its thorny exterior, disagreement arrives bearing beautiful gifts. We'll end here with a love letter that illustrates what healthy handling of conflict can do for us.

Dear constructive conflict,

We've known you all our lives.

We watched our elders acknowledge that you're vital to communication, or refuse to.

You were always present in our homes and schools.

You will always be part of our work lives and personal relationships.

You help us find our beliefs and push us to lift our voices for causes that matter.

You reveal others' unique positions when we're brave enough to listen.

Without you, we'd never admit that we see the world from one limited perspective, our own.

Because of you, we've learned our way is not the only way, there's often more than one way.

You remind us that those we see as dead wrong or out to get us may have positive intentions.

You bring anguish at times, anger and shouting—but you should not be confused with abusive communication. You have the power to restore harmony.

You allow emotional release when we can't find a solution and tears arrive.

You encourage us to find coaches and counselors to guide us through rough waters.

You help us identify our purpose.

You encourage tough discussions that lead to higher ground with coworkers, friends, enemies, strangers, and families.

You're inescapable.

You're a worthy puzzle that requires brain and heart working together to solve.

You shape our workplace culture.

You shape our family dynamics.

You're never the same thing twice.

You keep us growing as communicators, and we're grateful.

Love,
Michelle

CHAPTER 6 Pro Move

Why hold on to issues you've never taken the risk to air out? Find courage to request a conversation rather than choosing to run from disagreements or jump into them with boxing gloves. Consider your five options (compete, avoid, accommodate, compromise, or collaborate) and choose a method that fits the situation and your desired outcome rather than automatically engaging in your go-to style.

Think about a recent conflict you experienced. Name it: What conflict style did you use? Would another have served you better?

CHAPTER 6 Exercise

At the top of a fresh clean page, name the topic of a recent disagreement you have now or had in the past with another person. Under that topic, title one column "ME" and the next column "THEM." Now, list a few respectable points of each position. (It's usually easier to come up with good points of your own position.) Bravely take the risk to give their position some credit. Your ego is not always your amigo, so you may need to ask it to stand down as you consider the points you list under "THEM."

From here, you have something you respect about the other's position to speak aloud. This may help them in turn listen to you. It creates higher ground. Examples: "We both love our kid more than anything but disagree about where to send him to school," "We both want this project to succeed but disagree about approach," "We both want to be heard but keep interrupting one another." Forge ahead, and hopefully the vibe will change from *you vs. me* to *us vs. the problem.*

Hidden Challenge #4: Settling for "Good Enough"

STAND AND BE COUNTED

The fullness of life is in the hazards of life.

—EDITH HAMILTON, FIRST FEMALE STUDENT
AT THE UNIVERSITY OF MUNICH, GERMANY

OUR FINAL HIDDEN CHALLENGE to unearth and do something about is a common tendency to do just enough to get by in communication. The risk to stretch beyond Settling may be acceptable once weighed, yet we don't invest ourselves as much as we could. This avoidance is not new; it connects all four hidden challenges.

When we're Hiding from Risk, we avoid seeing our weak spots so we duck out of feedback. When we're Defining to Be Right, we avoid admitting bias or are overly sure of ourselves, which limits our inclusiveness.

When we're Rationalizing the Negative, we avoid believing things can go well even in difficult communications.

When we're Settling for "Good Enough," we avoid extending ourselves, so we miss unexpected wins and joys.

Settling is thinking "I'll do the minimum to get by" in a situation where we have more to add as communicators but choose not to, and we sell ourselves short. I've noticed avoidance when asking people about their communication fears in research for this book. This has not been a popular topic. People seem annoyed by the question and not eager to answer. Understandable. An answer to "What scares you related to communication?" requires an honest look at oneself and a willingness to admit vulnerability, something many see as a weakness rather than a strength.

DON'T SELL YOURSELF SHORT BY SETTLING

This final hidden challenge is taking the seemingly easy road in the short term. Settling is *satisficing*: a combination of doing what suffices and is satisfactory, perhaps because one may lack a sense of purpose to propel them. They might sit back, comfy in their comfort zone, willing to let their team or family do the heavier lifting with communication. They are not as valued, rewarded, or depended upon as a result. People stuck in the Settling rut may need to consider that although they haven't been given many communication-related assists in life to date, they can role-model the effort they wish others had expended for them.

When we're in this satisficing mode, we may think "I'll let the talkative people talk" rather than participate. We sure as heck aren't investing fully in ourselves as communicators. We can't quite find the impetus to represent our positions or others' positions with verve.

People often have excuses about why they're not trying in situations where more effort is needed. Deep down, they want to motivate themselves to apply more effort. They subscribe to the myth that good enough when writing, teaming, presenting, listening, speaking, or giving feedback is good enough. They often confide in me that they believe doing nothing is a neutral stance. In reality, it's often a negative influence on everyone.

I'm not advocating that you bend over backwards to the point that your communication or service to others exhausts you. You have a right to say no, or to offer limited involvement if a request does not align with your priorities, or is someone else's emergency. We're talking about situations where you lay low but have more to give, and you know it. You suspect if you try to do more than required as a communicator in some situations, it might blow up in your face. It might not go well. It may create a mess of some sort. Even so, that outcome can present an upside. You can't make this kind of stuff up, the screwups that inevitably happen when we least expect it. And you can use those learning moments to become a more persuasive communicator as you take the risk to share your less-than-shining moments.

I've facilitated thousands of training events. Adults learn best when they participate, so I'm on a never-ending quest to draw comments, answers, and questions out of audiences no matter what topic I'm teaching. It's interesting to me how often in the post-training evaluations, when asked what could make training better, people suggest "more participation." I agree, and would need many of those respondents to decide to personally step up to participate. Think about it. Have you attended any team meetings where comments and questions were encouraged, but the invitation to engage was met with silence—*your* silence? Were you settling for the sad rationalization that if no one else is speaking up, why should you? As author Dennis Covington puts it:

> There are moments when you stand on the brink of a new experience and understand that you have no choice about it. Either you walk into the experience or you turn away from it, but you know that no matter what you choose, you will have altered your life in a permanent way.

OUTSMART THE URGE TO SETTLE

Raise your hand and risk letting us hear what you have to say, diplomatically whenever possible. You get out of most communication what you put in to it. Your lived experience will be there for you and others as one of your greatest teaching tools. In retelling your stories, you get to savor any courage you show as a communicator. Added bonus: your mind keeps chewing on *Pro Moves* long after you try them. Meanwhile, we get to learn from your courageous willingness to share what didn't go as well as you'd hoped.

Sharing goes both ways as we risk communication investments in others. We face choices daily about whether to explicitly acknowledge emotions that others express nonverbally. It takes courage to ask others about feelings. Can you recall the last time you noticed a signal of emotion from someone, then asked about it? Alisa Yu, Justin Berg, and Julian Zlatev's research about the social implications of verbally acknowledging others' emotions was published in the journal *Organizational Behavior and Human Decision Processes* in 2021. They found the act of addressing how someone feels ("You seem upset" or "You seem happy") increased interpersonal trust, a cornerstone of healthy relationships.

Inquiring to show you care is a *Pro Move* that earns trust. There's a cost to you, the perceiver, in terms of finite personal resources like time, energy, and attention to respond to answers containing negative emotions, but can be well worth it. These studies also showed that people prefer to have their emotions mislabeled as positive rather than negative. This reminds me of hearing "you look tired today" from someone observing me. What if I've never felt better? We both might be a little embarrassed about your assumption. It's wise not to draw conclusions so quickly that we forget to be careful with phrasing, but don't let that bit of extra effort stop you from inquiring. Your courage and goodwill are noticed when you open the door for others to self-disclose. It builds trust when you listen to someone who wants to vent or finds the courage to speak their needs.

GET IN THE GAME AS A COMMUNICATOR

I told some football fanatic friends that I planned to sprinkle a few sports analogies in this book. They warned me about clichés like "the one-yard line," etc. No problem. In Indianapolis Colts country, outside linebacker Darius Leonard's communication is anything but cliché. We've got several players with *Pro Moves* to look up to (just try to get Jonathan Taylor to brag one iota about himself), but the way Darius expresses himself is in a class by itself. He recently celebrated a teammate's accomplishment with a full body dance move I had to jump up and try. His courage, skill, and passion for his purpose come through in his communication.

After a commercial break in a Colts home game against the Patriots, the announcers summed up key plays per usual before we turned our attention to the next play. Just before the snap, one announcer jumped in: "And Darius Leonard is BACK IN THE GAME." His voice tone alone said volumes: this player is a force to be reckoned with, a game-changer. He decides what energy he wants to bring to workplace interactions, and boy, does he bring it. I want to live long enough and work hard enough to have someone say, "And Michelle Gladieux is back at the meeting," meaning "look out people, when she comes to the table, expect positive action to occur." See how it sounds with your name inserted. And good job, Darius. Thanks for taking risks and not being afraid to show off your joy.

I'll share one more NFL story. A few years ago, I met with a Seattle Seahawk who wanted coaching to orchestrate a career change. I was stuck in Defining mode. I accepted the work but harbored doubt that he would work as hard as my "regular" clients, thinking maybe his impressive sports status would mean he'd expect me to do most of the work. I was dead wrong. His work ethic was outstanding. And why wouldn't it be? Look at the heights he reached in his first career, football! I'm sharing this with you because (1) admitting my bias is an exercise in vulnerability, and (2) so I'm less likely to prejudge someone again based on their achievements or lack thereof.

On any given day, folks in our coaching programs are in the middle of executing goal plans containing *Pro Moves* to help them take brave risks. These are regular people, leaders like you and me. One of the attributes that makes them a leader is the simple fact they recognize their action or inaction impacts self and others. We call what we do "executive" coaching not because we only work with C-suite clients but because we *all* deserve to be treated like executives. All of us should enjoy the feeling of people being respectful when they speak to us.

Coaching program participants meet with me a few hours each month, then I cook up a goal plan including five to eight personalized "to dos" to build their courage and risk-taking ability as communicators. These are action items, steps to take to grow that may bring up some fear worth facing. Once participants approve their monthly goal plan, they've given their word they'll carry it out. Here's a sample of some of the courageous communication going down these days, likely in an organization near you!

Real-Life Growth Goals from Real-Life Clients' Goal Plans:

o You report feeling scattered and not able to give your personal best to current projects. Complete a "brain dump," listing all tasks on one page. Label each task as A, B, or C importance. Begin as soon as you prioritize the list to complete As first, then Bs, etc. This means less worrying about wasted time. Start showing up fully for things you say "yes" to or look at your list and say "no" where you can. Tip: "C" priorities are good for delaying, delegating, or declining.

o Answer these 4 Amazing Questions to highlight what you won't be "Settling" about in the year ahead: (1) What do I like most about my communication style? (2) What do I like least? (3) What would I most like to see change? (4) What baby steps would help me start that change, and what help can I ask from others to make it more likely I'll pull it off?

o Be aware of your energy in important interactions. Strive to make it real, uplifting, and positive. This doesn't mean you can't acknowledge tough issues or confront dysfunction. Do so as quickly as possible, if possible, and do so respectfully.

o Play with stating your intention as a communicator more often. It warms up your tone so others don't perceive disapproval or judgment unless that's what you intend to project. Body language counts, too, so align your mind and body with your words.

o Develop a professional communication creed so you
   know what you will stand for and speak out about.
   This can also include what you will say "no" to, when
   appropriate.

o Name someone who may be deserving of an apology from
   you for communication mistakes. No matter how tardy the
   apology, it's never "too late" as long as you can still locate
   the person. You may want to use a preamble that explains
   that you've been thinking more lately about how you've
   come across in the past, and that you want to be better.

o Watch for chances to specifically compliment your most
   challenging coworker or family member when you see
   them approximating behaviors you appreciate.

o Your definition of success is largely other-based. Your
   affirmation for a job well done comes more from others
   than it does from within yourself. It sidelines your own
   opinions of your work. For balance, author a one- or two-
   sentence definition of success for a few important roles in
   your life. The only opinion that counts in this exercise is
   your own. These definitions will help you communicate
   more confidently and lower stress.

o Here's a mindset challenge since you shared you're
   confident only when you know something for certain. Tell
   yourself "When I don't know something for certain, I can
   handle that and will learn more to gain knowledge power—
   so I'm still confident." Choose to believe in your ability to
   admit what you don't know (a *Pro Move* that many of us
   miss), to ask questions, and to be an interested learner. This
   allows you to be more relaxed in any situation.

o Start working on a growth plan for yourself. On the
   right side of one page, list what you need to learn.
   Good sources of "need to learn" information can

include formal input such as past performance reviews or informal input from those in your inner circle. On the left side of the page, list HOW you might learn that entry and a reasonable goal date to be able to demonstrate proficiency in that topic. Extra credit if you begin a list of people, experiences, and educational materials that may be useful.

As you overcome one less-helpful habit and replace it with a healthier communication habit, do not grow complacent. Don't think you've got your challenges completely licked. Often, hidden challenges reemerge in new forms. This is why I describe fear as a shape-shifter. For example, after many years of struggling with the bad habit, I can now (mostly) stop myself from interrupting even when I disagree. My passion used to get in my way, but I'm gaining impulse control. You, too, can benefit from thinking through your strengths (such as a passionate approach to communication) and analyzing what the downsides can be if not properly managed.

Although I'm getting a handle on my interrupting habit, when the person finishes their thought, I might lead with "Well, here's how you're wrong . . ." Isn't that (Defining) pleasant? Of course, it's not. When I defeat one challenge, it often morphs into another. You never graduate fully from the pursuit of hidden challenges. I've done some introspection, which I highly recommend. If I can do it, so can you, but it can be uncomfortable to think about family norms. My family enjoys debate but there was no room for spouting off with incorrect information. You'd get called out swiftly. Life experience taught me that retorts common at our dining room table don't play as well with communicators outside that environment. I'm learning!

My competitiveness—a strength and weakness in one trait—is something else I've become more introspective about in recent years. I enjoy contests. There is a contest in communication, but it's less about us against others and more about competing against ourselves. I asked my friend Paul (a terrific golfer, one of those guys who can play 36 holes and still be up for another round) to tell me about the competition he experiences playing against opponents in important tournaments. He was quick to educate me about the importance of playing against *the course* more than against other golfers, and I think it applies well to communication, too. Rather than one-upping others, let's look at ways we can achieve our personal best as communicators. This moves us further away from Settling.

Here's the deal. When we're in Settling mode, it's one of two things that impede our progress. We either don't have the ability to try, or we're unwilling to learn. The stopper is either willingness or ability. If I'm being candid, I respect those with less ability in any situation a whole lot more. At least if they try, they might learn.

CHAPTER 7 Pro Move

Test the power of one person: you. Instead of thinking, "It's not that important" or "I'm only one person," try: "I have the power to at least try to change this circumstance."

History is filled with people who made a difference by being first to act or by acting alone. Take a risk. Be the person who asks the first question or volunteers to say more than is required. Take the risk of being seen, misjudged, and misunderstood. You may happily find you are instead fairly judged, and even understood more fully. Be the person who holds hope and takes action.

CHAPTER 7 Exercise

You're probably demonstrating some courageous new behaviors that feel pretty authentic and comfortable if you completed some of the exercises at the end of Chapters 1 through 6. Let's up the ante now. Choose two challenges from the list of real-life clients' growth goals in Chapter 7. Be brave in your experimentation and be flexible so you can learn from the results.

It would be a *Pro Move* to tell people you've got an assignment to complete the challenges you choose. Providing some context and backstory will make it easier for you to venture outside your comfort zone. This makes it easier for them to support your growth. Remember, it can seem scary to your family, friends, or team when you take risks to grow, because growth always means something's changing.

CHAPTER 8

Risks Not Worth Taking

CHOOSE YOUR RISKS BEFORE THEY CHOOSE YOU

Keep your nose clean.

—DAD GLAD (MY FATHER, WARNING ME WHEN
I WAS A KID NOT TO JUMP INTO RISK
WITHOUT SOME FORETHOUGHT)

KEEP TAKING RISKS, by all means. Stand and deliver a toast at the next wedding you attend if you feel moved to do so. But don't take the risk of drowning your nerves by getting good and drunk before you give the toast. Some risks in communication are just not worth taking.

Don't risk your sanity by engaging with manipulative or unethical people. You may someday find yourself in a relationship with a duplicitous individual who doesn't deserve compromise, accommodation, or collaboration. Maybe you already are in such a relationship. You have my empathy. As British author Elizabeth David wrote, "There are people who take the heart out of you, and there are people who put it back." It feels awful when you put in good-faith effort and another person withholds it.

From the five styles of conflict in Chapters 4 and 6, this leaves you with avoiding or competing as communication options. Remove yourself (avoid) or set rules (compete) if you choose to or have to communicate with someone who reveals themself to be damaging to your health or spirit.

I'm a huge advocate of do-overs and second chances especially in tough communications, but when you know or strongly suspect someone's not trustworthy, they are worthy of avoidance. Here are a few rules of thumb that clue us in to someone's lack of trustworthiness, especially if these behaviors show up as a pattern of behavior: undermining other's opportunities or reputation, demonstrating manipulation such as leveraging guilt to get one's way, refusing responsibility for mistakes or hurts caused with attempts to shift blame.

It's OK to hold the line on your position or avoid communication with someone entirely. Don't spend too much precious time sweating it. Wish them well and move on. In the very few times I've done this, it was not done rashly or easily, but I'm glad it was done. Saying "goodbye" and meaning it is a somber but important *Pro Move* we occasionally need to reach for in our toolboxes.

MORE RISKS NOT WORTH TAKING

Don't risk setting unachievably high standards. Helen Keller, American author and activist, wrote that "one can never creep when one feels an impulse to soar." But not every impulse to soar as a communicator should be obeyed. We can be aware of our common human desire to orchestrate perfect outcomes. Visualization is effective in helping you pull off wins with courageous communication. But risk rarely leads to things going exactly as you visualize. Sometimes our ambition can get in the way of showing ourselves grace when results are less than ideal. Think "I need to practice," not "I need perfection."

If you have high expectations, I salute and join your pursuit of excellence. The downside is that we make life harder for ourselves and others as we struggle to accept that we mess up sometimes. It's beautifully human to achieve less than A+ outcomes when taking worthy risks as communicators. Perfection is an unattainable goal, a sure route to burnout. Please be gentle with yourself and others. Don't keep score about your wins and losses when it comes to getting outside your comfort zone.

The situation you're in reminds me of the Bob Dylan song "Love Minus Zero/No Limit." In it, Dylan sings the praises of a lover who views failure as a success, among other beautiful traits like being as true as ice, or fire. No book, no coach, no class, no person, *nothing* is going to polish your communication as well as the old-fashioned method of try, fail at some part of the interaction, and try again—maybe even when interacting with the same person the very next day. That's actually a pretty fair descriptor of the dynamics in most committed relationships, isn't it? You keep showing up, as do they.

Your act of trying is in itself a success. Do you see all the people not trying? Do your best when you do something new and let the rest go; make a plan to do better next time. In a recent coaching session with a client passionately attuned to her mission, I dared her to put her new communication intention where she could see it. She came back with temporary tattoos for both of us, probably due to our equal need for this intention. They say LET IT GO in a slanty, scripted font. I wore mine on my inner arm for our next session and for the week it was visible, I was a little more understanding of myself and others.

Letting others define you leaves you holding the short end of the stick in interactions. Give yourself a hand up instead. Figure out what success means to you, then live toward it as much as possible. I'm not sure why so many people have time to be critical of you when they could be working on themselves, but maybe that's just them choosing the path of least resistance. It's easier to rate others rather than looking for our own hidden challenges and routing them out.

Today I found a photo of myself at 23 years old. Fresh out of grad school, I had just nabbed an adjunct professor gig teaching organizational psychology. The students who enrolled had up to 30 years of life and work experience that I did not, could not. This could have led them to define me as incapable. What a wonderful opportunity to face fear and take a risk to succeed despite doubts that had to be present in my students' minds when I walked in. I talked to my dad before heading to campus my first time teaching that course. I was nervous about my young age compared to my adult students'. He reminded me: "They don't have to like you; they have to learn from you. Make damn well sure they learn something from you." Sweet, sweet perspective! Most of us want to be liked, but it's a *Pro Move* to consider the cost of the popularity contests we find ourselves joining.

Staying away from constructive or negative feedback limits your growth as a communicator and as a human. The difference between constructive and negative feedback is not that important if you develop a thicker skin. Constructive feedback is delivered gracefully, with some positives about your performance included like a spoonful of sugar to help the medicine go down. Negative feedback happens when the sender doesn't bother with balance, and instead just lays what you didn't do well on the line. Either way, seeking a kernel of truth that you can admit to and work on leaves you better and stronger for having heard it. Don't run from feedback. Don't risk losing the learning.

Quick story from real life this week: a close confidante pointed out (more like blurted out, in frustration) that I've been complaining a lot lately. This hurt to hear. My ego immediately ran to my aid: "They don't understand how hard you've been working, how much is on your shoulders! They don't appreciate you!" I introduced a second voice to debate my defenses: "OR, this person does appreciate you and notices you've been licking your wounds and forgetting to be grateful for the good in your life . . . and they care enough to point it out to you." I put the internal debate aside and started a coaching session with a nursing home leader. As is standard practice, I asked her what she's enjoying most and least about her work these days. Most? Making a difference in residents' lives. Least? Some staffers' tendencies to complain. "Oh," I said, "Isn't that the worst? Complaining can be such a negative influence . . ." Yes, I heard myself. Yes, I'm working on it.

Staying in a negative, adverse employment situation for too long can be damaging to your health. If your attempts to improve the culture where you work or volunteer don't yield any movement toward wellness, take some steps to get out of there before you succumb to burnout. Polish your job search tools, line up references, research job openings, and begin to confide in trustworthy people that you're open to other employment. I've seen these self-advocating acts drastically reduce stress in people even as they continue to work where they'd rather not.

Communicating when you're too angry to see clearly is not a *Pro Move*; I know you know. You have much more to lose than gain in this scenario. Better to vent accusations and insults on paper and then watch it burn rather than draft an email and accidentally or intentionally hit "send." This reminds me of something comedy legend Carol Burnett said—that "words, when printed, have a life of their own." It also reminds me of a worthy communication challenge my significant other recently suggested. He pointed out that during high-stress communication (when we're arguing), we could separate ourselves from engaging at all. "Let's take a few minutes or maybe even an hour break to let our brain juices work through our drive to entrench ourselves in our positions, so we can see a more complete picture." Mic drop! What a great idea. It's hard for us both because of our competitive natures, but it's something I am finding the courage to try.

Watch for what bothers you most about others, by the way. That's some smart sleuthing, courageous and rare. Those "difficult people" may get your goat simply because you haven't yet admitted you're like them in some way that would feel "ick" to you. "You can find on the outside only what you possess on the inside," Adolfo Ballesteros, a Uruguayan writer, cautions us about this form of blindness.

Trying to be funny when you might instead be insulting is also not a risk worth taking. Negativity and criticism resonate deeply and longer with message recipients than praise likely ever will. The most commonly uttered words of defense for workplace harassment are, "I was just joking." It's worth a second thought if that overused statement is in your repertoire. Consider whether (or not) your humor is welcome.

"Watch it, buddy." Don't get yourself into a fisticuffs situation in a roadside bar when standing up to a bully just because you have a goal to take more risks after reading this book. Here's why I say that: it's interesting to watch coaching clients who usually hang back start to take risks to build their directness or confidence. Many people turn their risk dial from 2 to 10 instead of from 2 to 3. Baby steps work best. 2 to 10 is a jump I don't recommend.

That's how it is when we get a new tool in our hands. We need to gauge where, when, and how to use the tool, including risk-taking. I remember the first eye shadow I ever purchased by myself with babysitting money. It was my favorite color and still is to this day—bright turquoise blue. I wore it to ballet class, from lid to brow, really painted on. My older, wiser neighbor gal pal gave me a ride to class, and looked at my face. "Did you get some new eye shadow?" she asked. Talk about a diplomatic communicator. Don't overdo.

Assuming people know how you feel about them. One more night. One more road trip. One more laugh, joke, picnic, embrace, hockey game, theater performance, spin around the dance floor, walk on the beach, trip to the grocery store, text, talk on the phone, or opportunity to ask or give advice . . . you realize everyone you hold dear will someday be unable to attend to life's moments with you, right? Muster up your courage. Pop a note in the mail. If you don't love snail mail as much as I do, that's OK. Drop a quick line via electronic means to share your gratitude for what makes the standout people in your life uniquely special.

Time waits for no one, and all the money in the world can't buy you one more day with your favorite people when they move on. This applies to our animals, too. The four fur babies (Angel, Marley, Janie, and Neil Young) I've had to bid goodbye? At least those pups heard many dozens of times per week how smart, needed, appreciated, and stunningly handsome and beautiful they were. If only we spoke as generously to our humans as we do our pets, they'd really feel seen.

It's a *Pro Move* to go out of your way to demonstrate others' value early and often. The longer we wait to hear from you, the less we assume we matter. My editor, Jeevan, understands this and has applied it to his email communication for 23+ years with no signs of stopping. He responds to everyone within 24 hours 99% of the time, a stretch goal worth consideration.

A FEW MORE RISKS NOT WORTH TAKING

Nagging is a poor communication strategy. It risks others losing tolerance for your messaging. It rarely works, and it doesn't feel good to engage in it. A better approach is to acknowledge your needs and seek ways to meet them, independently if necessary.

Not keeping confidential communication confidential limits others' ability to trust you with sensitive information. Like complaining, leaking a secret has a certain natural high to it, until the thrill is gone and you're left with the negative impact on your reputation as a communicator. The cons outweigh the pros of the dopamine hit one gets from sharing a secret.

Bullshitting is usually not a risk worth taking. Yes, sometimes it works out, but not as often as bullshitters would like. It's especially no good for presentation situations. "Oh, what a tangled web we weave, when first we practice to deceive." That wasn't Shakespeare. It was Sir Walter Scott, a Scottish novelist, playwright, poet, and historian. He's right. It's a lot of work trying to remember who you told what to. Save yourself the trouble.

Summing up, uncalculated communication risks are where things get dicey. Size up the challenge so you don't shoot before you aim. Never underestimate what practice + planning + daring can do.

CHAPTER 8 Pro Move

Exercise restraint when a risk's cons outweigh its potential pros. Hold your horses. Don't be so eager to show off your courage to take risks that you fail to size up chances of success or to calculate the possible cost of your communication goals.

CHAPTER 8 Exercise

Evaluate your modus operandi (M.O.) as a communicator. Where might you need to rein in some risk? It could be in the way you address someone by first name instead of using the honorific (Doctor, Captain, Coach) before you have their permission. It could be as simple as not risking an assumption is understood by all: "I'll risk not answering this email. They already know I care." And maybe we do, but we still might appreciate a response.

CHAPTER 9

The Most Important Conversations to Have

YOUR WORDS HAVE POWER

The single biggest problem in communication is the illusion that it has taken place.

—GEORGE BERNARD SHAW,
IRISH PLAYWRIGHT

OUR COMPANY ADVERTISES at our hometown airport near an upstairs boarding gate. The sign features a road winding through green pastures. We ask travelers, "Where are you headed?" on the sign, because we think it's a worthy question. Where are you headed?

Living your purpose and living up to your potential means taking an honest look at how you speak and write, and to whom. Have you noticed people talk a lot about how others come across, but it's the rare few who manage their own interactions with such a close eye? When I get lazy about exercise, my fitness trainer Kevin encourages me: "Get 15 minutes in today. Something is better than nothing!" The same goes for communication. If we don't exercise these muscles, they atrophy. If there are conversations you've been meaning to have, get going. Reach out to offer the compliment, ask your question, or address the conflict. It may feel awkward. The first 60 seconds are usually the hardest. The risk is worth it, because you're awakening parts of you and your life that deserve to be alive. You might wake some of the rest of us up as well.

SHOWING UP FOR OTHERS

With *Pro Moves* in our toolkits, we're equipped to really show up for interactions. As communicators, we can often improve a situation in more ways than we realize. How we show up moderates the quality of life we'll have going forward. It affects those most important to us as well. There's a woman in my neighborhood, Fran, who has known me since I was a lanky teenager. I took piano lessons and tried to teach what I was learning to one of her daughters after each class. She often included me in family dinners. She and her husband Steve created a warm home in walking distance that you wouldn't ever want to leave. Fran really shows up as a communicator. No matter how long it's been between our conversations, she inserts, "I love you, Shelly!" (The nickname I chose as a kid still lingers with folks who've known me the longest.) She speaks it like a gift she hopes others will accept. I love her, too, and can say so, but this act of courage always floors me. She goes first with sharing feelings. It's courage that lets her wear her heart on her sleeve. Her bravery shines a light on others' lives. Her communication choices remind me of something the author Leo Buscaglia said: "Too often we underestimate the power of a touch, a smile, a kind word, a listening ear, an honest compliment, or the smallest act of caring, all of which have the potential to turn a life around."

Some not-to-be-missed conversations include: advocating for self and others, establishing accountability via performance feedback, recognizing others' efforts and accomplishments, promoting inclusion, asking forgiveness, setting expectations, choosing and using goals, practicing honesty, negotiating for improved outcomes, expressing emotion, sharing stories and struggles, announcing change, mentoring, and check-ins with the person you speak to the most—that's yourself, about what you sense and need.

I've dated some great guys who had to endure my wanting to communicate about relationship stuff longer than they would have preferred. From teen years on, I was more into analyzing communication than most people had patience for. I hope I've gained some emotional intelligence. I think I finally understand that not everyone has the same tolerance for tough conversations, and some conversations need to end earlier, especially if they're not going anywhere, or if either party is fatigued.

If you hate talking about relationship stuff, maybe stay in the conversation a little longer, as a growth and empathy exercise. If you enjoy such discussions, you can find growth by changing the subject a bit sooner when interacting with someone who seems uneasy or wants to be done with the communication.

Not only length, but pacing is relevant in our most important conversations. How do you know if you should look for opportunities to slow your roll as a communicator? If you move fast and like to see how many things you can get done in a day, it's likely you miss opportunities to listen, learn, collect, and understand feedback. You've got an "action bias," a preference for acting rather than waiting. There's a framed Gandhi quote in my living room which reminds me: "There is more to life than increasing its speed." Amen! I hope to fully internalize and master that message someday.

On the flip side, you may need to pick up the pace. You might witness a conversation or sit in a meeting, thinking of questions, points, counterpoints, and compliments, but the communication is over before you're in. Sadly, your contribution is lost due to your internal editor working overtime. Give it some time off and take the risk to speak, realizing you're probably as competent as the next person. If you're sure you're not, preface your contribution with a disclaimer: "I'm new to this group but . . ." or "I haven't thought this through entirely yet . . .", "I don't have all the data but I do know . . ." These preambles go a long way to make less vocal communicators more comfortable. The preamble is a *Pro Move* whether you're talkative, or not.

It's a *Pro Move* to address your most important conversations at the start of your day. That may be "I have a question," "I love you," "I'm sorry," or confronting a dysfunctional behavior someone is exhibiting. Diplomacy and directness are your best friends in challenging interactions. To use them best, blend them. Say the hard thing clearly but consider how it will leave the recipient feeling. This is tricky, like walking a tightrope, but we all get better with practice. Choose your words and remember that you can revise them when they don't land as you had hoped. Apologize if you veer too far into assertive style. You're going for "not a doormat" and at the same time "not a bully," a tough balance to strike. You might look at it the way American writer and poet Alice Duer Miller did: "If it's very painful for you to criticize your friends—you're safe in doing it. But if you take the slightest pleasure in it, that's the time to hold your tongue."

FIGURE OUT WHAT YOU'RE
HERE TO DO AS A COMMUNICATOR

Here's a very important conversation to have with yourself: Select a reason for being. If you don't feel connected to a purpose in your life or work, it's likely coming through in your communication content, tone, and delivery. To figure out your purpose(s), ask yourself what you're interested in doing, for or with whom, and what benefits can arise from your effort. After this talk with yourself about your unique mission, carve out time to be present in those pursuits. Living toward a purpose is a *Pro Move*. It silences mind chatter and allows you to be more present in everything you do.

One of my favorite places for gifting great food to myself and others is Zingerman's Deli in Ann Arbor, Michigan. They've been around since 1982 when Ari Weinzweig and Paul Saginaw got a $20,000 loan and put their restaurant experience to use, opening their doors with two employees and terrific sandwiches. With purpose at the fore, they've grown to 10 businesses, 750 employees, and well over 50 million dollars in annual revenue. They keep learning, they keep giving back, and I've never had a negative experience with them. They make mistakes, but they make things right. They've crafted a 2023 vision to aim for as they celebrate their 50th anniversary. Here's an excerpt: "We view everyone through the lens of a compassionate heart, choosing patience, positive beliefs, and pausing to appreciate the beauty in everyone and everything we work with. We are mindfully conscious of how our decisions impact the people we work with, our customers, and the larger community. We understand that the energy we put into every interaction is essential. We are self-reflective and intentional in our work in this way." Ari says that when they fall short, the goal is to take a deep breath and compassionately go forward, just as you and I must when we stumble in our most important interactions.

Say "no" to preserve your time and energy when you need to. Where you're able, use your voice to decline, delegate, or delay tasks to get more time to devote to activities that align with your purpose. Say "yes" when you have to (such as when your boss makes a request) and when your soul speaks. One coaching client with a terminal illness told me in a session, "My time is limited, Michelle, and I know it. So, I'm only saying 'yes' when it's a 'HELL, YES!'" Communicating with courage makes good use of your time. A great example of this time-saving effect is demonstrated by my colleague Christine when she extricates herself from communication that is no longer fruitful. She's a VP at Powered by Purple Ink, a network for people professionals. She meets and interviews many possible network partners. If it's not a fit, or if the conversation has reached its limit of usefulness for those involved, she'll suggest: "Let's give each other some time back." *Pro Move*: treat time expended to communicate like it matters, because it does.

There are many types of conversations to prioritize. Negotiation is a skill most of us will benefit from honing personally and professionally. Advocate for yourself when it comes to winning job offers, pay raises, better benefits, respect, title changes, project opportunities, or asking coworkers or friends/family to change a behavior that's detrimental to yourself or others.

Inquire. As we become better at lifting our voice with questions that benefit us, we become better at advocating for others with our questions. For example, as you get comfortable with asking medical providers about your health or treatment options, you can assist loved ones who may need a helping hand in a health-related scenario.

Speak to lift others up. You can probably feel it when someone's energy is off, if you're paying attention. That's when they might need some "pep in their step," as my friend Steve often says with gusto. Let's raise a glass to friends who throw light, not shade. Cheers to them! Cheers to you, and to Steve, for being that kind of friend as you take the risk to engage.

Ask if you can give some feedback, an opinion that could help another grow. There's a Russian proverb that makes me think of some chosen and biological family who never shy from a debate: "A mere friend will agree with you, but a true friend will argue."

Ask for time to think when you need it. A *Pro Move* in conversation is to demonstrate respect for your own and others' need to concentrate. Kindly ask for space to be productive or creative: "I need to focus on this, so please give me an hour," for example. Offer the same courtesy to others: "Is this a good time to ask you a few questions?"

Many of our most important conversations occur during times of significant change. Mike Amundson, the company president at Quality Refrigerated Services requested we check in with his employees working from home in Omaha, Nebraska, as a stress-preventative measure during the pandemic. He's also personally doing so. He is aware (a *Pro Move*) that disruption to usual ways of working often means more coaching support is needed. He and the rest of the leadership team have decided they will care about their employees personally as well as professionally—they know what they want to do with their communication. So, to learn how the at-home team members experienced the up and down sides of the change, our survey included:

> Is your employer clearly communicating next steps to you?
>
> Do you have someone to talk to from work or personal life?
>
> Have you and your coworkers been provided tools you need to do your job effectively?
>
> Have you learned any new skills or ways of doing things as a result of this change?

What's been challenging or stressful about this new way of working?

What hasn't changed? For what are you grateful that continues?

Maybe it's time for you to adopt some new ways to communicate, too. Your personality (consistent thoughts, motivations, and priorities) offers clues about what will work for you.

If you're analytical, you need to think about things deeply. Allow quiet time to study, read, or visualize outcomes you're seeking.

If you're expressive, you inspire and are inspired by others. Share the reasons behind the change, your concerns, and possible benefits of the change. Let your relationship skills help you engage even when the waters get rough.

If you're amiable, you're a true team player who strives to achieve harmony. You can benefit from focusing on courage to face change and participate in tough conversations.

If you're a driver, you're assertive and you need task completion. You will enjoy taking an immediate small step toward what's new. You prefer to have important conversations without delay.

When you're the change agent or announcing a change, you can take steps to make it easier on others:

- Talk face-to-face. Avoiding doing so because you're avoiding dealing with their responses is a common mistake that undermines your credibility.
- Show respect for the flow you're interrupting. Do so by explaining reasons driving the change.
- Engage others in looking at the problem before forming solutions, so they see the trade-offs required to move forward.

- Answer questions honestly to prevent rumors. Say, "I don't know" if you don't.
- Take small first steps immediately to prevent fear from immobilizing people.

A fellow named Matt Kelley is one of my favorite change agents and courageous communicators. He's the owner of One Lucky Guitar, a boutique creative agency that helps client organizations communicate brand soul. He's a leader of the band who beta-tested a Team Check-In during pandemic separation. He's so magnanimous he considered naming a band Magnanimous—he is focused on the greater good. This is probably why he listens well. Matt gives more than is required to build his community. For example, he launched—he'd want me to say with lots of help from other people—the Middle Waves Music Festival and brought new life to his hometown. He holds steadfast to his values to guide his way. He helps client companies do the same. He communicates his vision and rallies people around it. He moves daily toward his best communication self.

Your potential as a communicator moves toward you as you move toward it. "What you seek is seeking you" is how the 13th century Persian poet Rumi stated this phenomenon. If you manage communication strategically with emotional intelligence, you have more time for soul-filling pursuits and less time to worry.

WHY EMOTIONAL INTELLIGENCE DESERVES YOUR ATTENTION

There's a lot of talk, research, and writing these days about emotional intelligence. What a boon to all of us that we're tuning in to this frequency. This is a type of social intelligence you use to monitor your own and others' feelings, then allow that information to guide what you think and say. Building your emotional intelligence is a truly *Pro Move*.

Emotional Intelligence (EI, often conflated with EQ) helps us express emotions, tend to relationships, and succeed in life and work. EQ is different from Intelligence Quotient (IQ) or personality. It bundles with personality and IQ to shape the way we speak and write. It impacts our communication style and preferences.

EQ is an exciting discovery of the past few decades, offering deeper understanding of our potential which can help us evolve. EQ fuels *Pro Moves*. In 1985, the term EI was coined by Dr. Reuven Bar-On, an Israeli psychologist. In 1989, it was introduced in scientific articles by Drs. Salovey and Mayer. In 1995, Dr. Goleman expanded on this work, which led to his book *Emotional Intelligence: Why It Can Matter More Than IQ*.

Emotional Intelligence helps us hold our most important conversations. We all need this resource, and anyone can build it. You don't need to be the smartest person in the room to enjoy its advantage. Did you know that people with average IQs are estimated to enjoy more success and deploy more effective communication than those with the highest IQs? And why is that? It's because they have two competencies that help them navigate social complexities.

- Personal competence: staying aware of emotions and tendencies
- Social competence: understanding others' moods and motives

EQ is a flexible set of skills that improve with practice. You can develop it if you aren't born with it, and even if your early caregivers didn't model it—isn't that a relief? As our EQ expands, we notice more of what's going on in interactions. Imagine what that might do for our nations, companies, teams, and families. We increasingly rely on technology as face-to-face interpersonal skills seem to be slipping away. Often, my team addresses this performance gap as conference presenters. It's always a happy challenge to share a bunch of tips in a short time, getting to the heart of *Pro Moves* before participants get back to their trade show.

A frequent theme running through our presentations about EQ regardless of audience, industry, or job type is "conduct an experiment." Taking on a new behavior (or letting go of an old, less useful one) has ripple effects that extend to each role you play in life. As you hold your most important conversations, you become more influential, more able to make a difference in situations that matter to you. You tune in to nuances. Hone some *Pro Moves,* and over time, and with practice, you could become exceptional at sending and receiving information. It's an ethical way to gain power.

Power comes from holding your most important conversations regardless of how they go. I enjoy teaching four types of power, each worth your time to expand. Small steps here net big results.

Personal power—How sincerely interested in others are you? Are you someone who we feel comfortable approaching with a question? To grow personal power: let others see you adapt to change by sharing some of your challenges.

Relationship power—How deep and wide is your network? How many people do you know, and how well? To grow relationship power: attend industry events online or in person and follow up with a few new acquaintances to continue the conversation if they're willing. Volunteer for a cause you believe in to expand your circle of influence.

Position power—How much decision-making authority do you have? To grow position power: be visible. Ask for projects or new areas of responsibility.

Knowledge power—How sharp is your expertise? Do you keep it growing? To grow knowledge power: ask questions to show your interest in others' expertise and work.

A fun way to empower yourself is to align with an intention. Rather than adopting a New Year's resolution to fall by the wayside before spring, I narrowed my focus this year to one word. It encourages me to use EQ to treat others as I'd like to be treated. It's "grace." My friend and visual designer Heather Shively suggested another word for me to use as my North Star—the musical term *fermata* (to hold or rest, an extended note). Bless her for knowing that I often need an extended pause to search about for my grace. And bless her for caring enough to ponder what intention might help me the most. This bonus communication in which she chose to engage is the opposite of Settling. It was and is a hand up on my climb to better communication.

EQ is essential to realizing your potential, whether you're leading family, volunteers, an organization, or yourself. If you have employees, your EQ affects how fulfilled people feel in your workplace. The Wilson Learning Corporation conducted a study of 25,000 employees in 14 organizations to investigate the link between business performance, employee satisfaction, and leadership practices. The findings: 39% of the variability in company performance was attributable to employees' job satisfaction. Then they wisely asked, "What factor is most important to predict job satisfaction?" Supervisors across the land, are you ready for this? 69% of variability in job satisfaction (employee fulfillment) was attributed to the leadership qualities *of the supervisor*! How a boss behaves really matters, and "soft skills"—a term I detest because it minimizes how hard it is to get great at communicating—can make or break workplaces.

According to a 2017 TalentSmart study, people with high EQ enjoy better pay annually. This holds true in all industries, at all levels, in every part of the world. Performance and pay are tied closely to EQ, but don't let money be your only motivator. Let your good name be your inspiration, and decide what you want to become known for. Try to boil what you want more of in your life down to its essence. This year (or perhaps more useful, this week) what intention calls to you? Consider tasty selections we've seen from training participants, or make up your own:

Abundance, Art, Balance, Belief, Commitment, Community, Concentration, Confidence, Courage, Creativity, Determination, Desire, Equality, Experience, Faith, Family, Freedom, Generosity, Goals, Gratitude, Growth, Happiness, Health, Honesty, Hope, Humor, Imagination, Independence, Integrity, Knowledge, Learning, Legacy, Motivation, Nature, Opportunity, Patience, Peace, Planning, Possibility, Potential, Power, Preparation, Progress, Purpose, Reliability, Risk, Self-Esteem, Service, Simplicity, Spirit, Teaching, Thriving, Transcending, Trust, Truth, Uplift, Value, Victory, Vision, Well-being, Will, Wisdom, Worth, Yearning, Zeal, Zest, Zen.

You can fold an intention into four ways to build emotional intelligence:

1. Strengthen self-awareness. Name your feelings as they happen.

2. Manage your emotional health by sticking to a healthy stress management habit. This can be anything that takes your mind off your worries to center and calm you.

3. Stoke your motivation to pay attention, delay gratification, or stifle impulsiveness.

4. Grow in empathy by asking open-ended questions to understand others' perspectives.

Eventually, you'll use *Pro Moves* more effortlessly and see yourself as others do when they're placing you in your best light. While it's valuable to know how you're perceived, I hope you won't always bow to the world's preferences. Your independent thought is valuable. Have the courage to risk feeling that others' opinions of your communication matter, but keep your opinion of how you send and receive messages clearly in view.

I've always loved the poem "The Summer Day" by Mary Oliver. In it, a grasshopper flings herself out of the grass to devour sugar in Mary's hand. The poem ends: "Doesn't everything die at last, and too soon? Tell me, what is it you plan to do with your one wild and precious life?"

You know what I'm going to suggest. Use your life to make the most of the gifts of communication. Show up for your most important conversations. Initiate them if no one else steps up to do so. Try to see beyond ethnicity, gender, age, and all the variables that make one human no less valuable than another. Thank those whose shoulders you stand on for the learnings they pass on to you. You have a wholly unique voice. You have limited time to use it, but unlimited opportunities to practice while you're here. You might as well try to pull off some *Pro Moves* with confidence and poise.

A comfort zone is a beautiful place, but nothing ever grows there.

—ANONYMOUS

In need of a break from work, I recently listened to a friend's song melody and was asked to suggest lyrics. Songwriters deeply feel the importance of words. I dig that. The tune sounded sad, so I penned a few lines about loss. What emerged—and quickly, isn't it a gift when you need words and that happens?—was about my mom, Rosemary, to whom this book is dedicated. The songwriter said he needed "a thematic chorus statement." My, that sounds fancy. I wasn't 100% sure what that meant, so I kept my chorus simple, remembering teenage arguments with my mom: "You fought me, and I fought you. But my best words are your words. They never fail to pull me through." I nod to this truth: much of the best stuff I teach to communicators like you, I learned from teachers like her. We pick up what we can from communicators we've known. Luckily, just as my teenage years ended and she was still here in physical form, we made progress with our communication. "Me vs. you" started to feel more like "us vs. our disagreements."

Progress is what you're after, too. In communication, it's usually two steps forward, one step back. Keep moving in a positive direction. Rest when you need to. You don't need to be courageous in every communication, but certainly in your most important communications, you want to be.

KEEP YOUR HEART IN WHAT YOU SAY AND HOW YOU SAY IT

Press "pause" for a few moments to visualize success for your most important communications before you begin them. You'll probably think of something you should (or shouldn't) have said afterward, but by summoning the courage to keep working at it, you are slowly becoming what you think about. And for now, you're right where you're supposed to be.

CHAPTER 9 Pro Move

Don't underestimate the power of emotion. Weave it into your most important conversations. Use your emotional intelligence and keep building it to help your communication be memorable, successful, and well-received.

CHAPTER 9 Exercise

Rate your use of each type of power (personal, relationship, position, and knowledge) from 1 (low) to 10 (high). Set an intention to grow in one of the four options. Get your growth mindset ready because there's a bit of magic in this exercise. What you seek is also seeking you. New opportunities are heading your way, and they'll arrive bearing unexpected gifts.

CHAPTER 10

The Complete Risk-Taking Communicator

RISK MORE, FEAR LESS

What you are will show, ultimately. Start now, every day, becoming, in your actions, your regular actions, what you would like to become in the bigger scheme of things.

—ANNA DEAVERE SMITH,
PROFESSOR AND PLAYWRIGHT

HOPE YOU'LL START TAKING more courageous communication risks daily or weekly to gain momentum. You'll start firing on all cylinders. Things will click in your communication that haven't before. You'll feel more fulfilled by messages you give and receive. People will disclose more than necessary when speaking with you. The way you approach your work and relationships will evolve. You'll find that trust shows up more abundantly in your interactions.

I currently work with one of the most exciting teams I've had the pleasure to know. Like every group of humans pursuing goals together, we have diverse backgrounds and wildly different personalities. No doubt that's helped us deploy some *Pro Moves* as we tackle a wide span of projects. When it comes to what a team needs to win and wow clients, for me, it's about trust. It's a risk to trust others because you may be hurt or let down by them. I don't give my trust away haphazardly, and don't advise you to do so, either.

Before I asked my coworkers to join my team, I imagined a do-or-die scenario. A pretend test. Mountain climbing with one of my colleagues, I lose my footing. I've never been mountain climbing, so this is no surprise! My survival could depend on this person. Could I count on them to give it their all and get creative if my life was on the line? If yes, then I'm inclined to trust them with our clients' well-being and our company's good name, because I'd trust them with my life.

The literal cliffhanger is of course not an easy test to pass. It may be a little extreme. But I've invested my life into this mission of raising people's game as communicators, and I don't want nagging doubts about anyone who pursues it with me. I admit it's much easier to trust coworkers when you get to do the hiring. When you're teaming with folks you didn't personally select, extending trust is easier if you make your expectations known and inquire about what they expect from you.

TEAM EFFECTIVENESS INCLUDES EMBRACING RISK

Imagine yourself at a half-day seminar. Your discussion group consists of three or four coworkers with whom you'll share your opinion about how you're doing—whether communication is happening and healthy. How does your current team rate when you offer your thoughts on these dimensions relating to courageous communication? (Each item in the inventory relates to taking risks as a communicator to build trust.)

- Purpose—Do we agree on why we exist? Will we take risks to achieve our goals?
- Training—Is learning valued in our culture and do we make it available to everybody?
- Decisions—Do we discuss who gets to decide and why? Are they clearly communicated?
- Conflict—Is it bravely addressed before it gets unnecessarily complicated?
- Personalities—Are diverse approaches understood, accepted, and acknowledged?
- Meetings—Are they worthwhile? Do we offer our opinions about how to make them more useful?
- Performance—Are fair, high standards upheld for all positions with no preferential treatment?
- Success—Is it celebrated? Do we wholeheartedly offer sincere praise to one another?

The *Pro Move*: run these questions by your real-life team. This gut-check yields discussion for teams from every type of organization. We see it spur useful goal setting. Many teams report feeling less stress after they talk about what's going right and what could be better.

Speaking of work stress, here's a question: Do you create any preventable stress for your team? Honest answer: Yes, you probably do, at least sometimes. It's a *Pro Move* to figure out how you (hopefully unintentionally) put glue in the gears. See if people trust you enough to answer when you ask. The Feedback Challenge exercise in Chapter 1 is a great tool for finding out how you're perceived. If you don't think people will be real with you, you need to earn more trust. There are ways to build it.

BUILDING TRUST

You won't always feel comfortable when you engage to build trust in new ways, but that's how learning mode is supposed to feel—a little scary. It's not straight-up fear, it's discomfort. At our company, it's learning mode when one of our quieter team members steps up to take the lead in a meeting. I'm in learning mode when I let others lead conversation while my DNA says, "Talk, girl!" Learning mode will always be somewhere between comfort zone and debilitating fear.

To build trust on a team, genuine communication is essential, as in any healthy relationship. In a study of 360 assessments, surveys seeking opinions from people inside and outside the organization involving 87,000 leaders (Zenger and Folkman, 2019), three variables stood out as trust-builders:

1. Positive relationships, real feedback delivered kindly, facing and resolving conflict together

2. Good judgment, derived from subject-matter expertise

3. Consistency, doing what you say you will or doing more than expected

To use risk-taking to build trust with others, you can also:

- Practice skillful self-disclosure. Revealing intentions, hopes, vulnerabilities, emotions, values, or goals at the right time to an appropriate extent lowers others' suspicions and lessens their feelings of distance from you.

- Limit "I" communication. Think, write, and speak "we." Honor others by sharing credit.

- Manage your personal brand. Document what you're known for (the good and not-so-good) and what you hope to be known for. Address one area needing attention today.

- Be truthful. What you can't share, acknowledge as confidential. This helps others trust you to keep private information to yourself.
- Bravely offer an apology for missteps or times you let people down. The short-term risk of looking bad because you failed is better than the long-term effects of blaming others.
- Increase face time in relationships. Email is a time-saver for sure but falls short when the topic calls for you to pair it with voice tone and facial expressions.
- Manage your dark moods with self-care so you don't lash out or drop out.

Patience is a *Pro Move* because trust-building works best over time and not with all colleagues. You're going to need it. People raised in a supportive environment reciprocate trust more easily. Early life experiences of isolation or uncertainty can interfere with development of a trusting personality as people may struggle to feel safe in relationships. And regardless of formative experiences, once someone lets us down, it's tough to trust them. Maya Angelou captured that "watch your back" thinking when she said, "When people show you who they are, believe them the first time."

To get a feel for whether trust is alive on your team, ask yourself:

1. Is my team proud to work together?

2. Do we enjoy collaborating?

3. Are people accountable to their word?

We gel with, vibe with, want to work with, get real with, and stand up for folks who stick by us, as we stick by them. At our company, we've learned from experience that self-imposed deadlines help us achieve our actual dreams. Our workplace arrangement doesn't allow as much face time as we'd like, and we work in different cities. If face time is sparse for you, too, put energy into collaboration to gain rewarding, feel-good cohesiveness. In whatever way you work together, the whole is greater than the sum of its parts when you combine diverse talents. Practice is necessary. I've heard it said you can't think your way into trust. You have to take a risk to give it. The *Pro Move* is to be known for keeping your word. Every time you do, your words gain power.

As we assess training needs for clients, teams sometimes share they have members no longer on speaking terms. Not ideal, certainly not with communication training approaching. It's hard to learn at the same time you're contemplating revenge or licking a wound. Us vs. them mentality is prevalent in Western workplaces, which is a shame. It's a drain on the culture, people, creativity, and of course, customers.

Workplace cliques happen because humans are social, political, and emotional creatures. Most want to work in harmony. Others enjoy drama and intentionally create it, the opposite of a *Pro Move*—unless, of course, you're aligned with the Dark Side.

If you're currently on a dysfunctional team, take tolerable, reasonable risks to improve your environment incrementally. Keep in mind what the essayist Ralph Waldo Emerson offers about risk: "Do the thing you fear and the death of fear is certain." Well, maybe not immediately certain, but the hard things we face as communicators do get easier to face with repeated attempts.

Start by examining how you interact with others. Is it easy to see who your favorites are? Each of us has most-preferred (in-group) and least-preferred (out-group) individuals. Productive communication with people you don't personally enjoy is part of your job. Let's say that once again louder for the people in the back. You don't have to want to spend your free time with everyone you have to communicate with, but you shouldn't lower your personal communication standards when dealing with less-preferred teammates. The more skilled you become at this, the less stressful life is.

Your out-group gets less attention, eye contact, time, genuine praise, and fewer open-ended questions like "What do you think?" or "How was your weekend?" from you. Take a few steps toward out-group members to try to improve those relationships. One coaching client in higher education is expanding use of praise by changing up the ways he recognizes others' effort. A leader at a hospital now spends 10 minutes a day asking what others need. A manufacturing operations manager is inviting quieter employees by name to offer opinions in meetings. Begin. You risk rejection, and that's OK.

Don't make the mistake of constantly evaluating what you get for what you give. Risk means giving more to your team, family, and self to see what happens. You win, too, because it's more fun to work on a happy, high-performing team and it's more enjoyable to be with family and friends when you're investing some effort.

CASE IN POINT: THE CLAM SHACK

Lackluster teams are everywhere. I'm looking at one now that is the exact opposite of lackluster. They're amazing. I'm at The Clam Shack, a restaurant in Sanibel, Florida, drawn in by the pull of live music. It's a creative, cool extra they don't have to offer but they choose to for customers' enjoyment. I look up from my delicious "lobstah" roll and notice genuine comradery between the owners (siblings) and staff. This same warmth greeted me at the door. There's always someone watching to see who enters and no one is too busy to greet people as they enter. The cook looks over, sneakily checking to see whether I'm enjoying my food. Although he knows my server will ask, he personally cares. My server takes initiative to share the musician's song request list with every table, to the musician's delight. Sister (Cara) grabs a song list and makes sure the cooks get a request in. Brother (Patrick) glides around the dining room asking each server, "What do you need?" I compliment his service to the servers. He replies that he hopes he's not bugging them, he just wants to help.

It's hard to tell who's in charge here because desire to serve and organizational citizenship behaviors are everywhere. Quick huddles and quiet, respectful conversations are held in small groups. Everyone hustles to make sure product and service are in harmony. It's holiday time. The restaurant is adorned inside and out to celebrate the season. Authentic team spirit is on display with New England Patriots signs reminding the community where this business was born. The décor is a touchstone to their mission: bringing delicious New England–style seafood to the Gulf Coast. I'm stating their mission in my own words, not theirs, but I'm confident they'd agree. Pictures of philanthropic events line the walls and feature their kids helping in the family business. The double shifts required in tourist season don't deflate their spirit or pride in their product. These folks have risked pursuing a dream and held nothing back. Good for them! And good for those who participate if only for one meal in the welcoming vibe created by a team that's got it going on.

Do you want some of what they've got? Yes, please! Here's a recipe for outstanding teamwork built on intelligent risks. You'll need a big pan.

Apply a thick coat of integrity (researchers Quade and Brown describe it: an allegiance to life-giving behaviors, behaving in a way that means more life for all) or things get sticky. You don't want team members fulfilling their own needs without regard for how others are affected. Stir in:

4 cups self-awareness

1 cup courage, to extend ourselves to others

1 cup humor, even on off-days

¾ cup cross-training so you can swoop in where helping hands are needed

½ cup effort to make others aware of how their behavior affects the team

½ cup vulnerability, so you can ask for constructive criticism and not expect perfection from self or others

Season generously with empathy and go to work with some love for what you do.

Hopefully, you now have a clearer picture of how capable risk-taking communicators behave.

Your classroom for smart risk-taking is everywhere you witness message sending and receiving. Consider any interaction and visualize what the person communicating with courage and heart would do. The courageous communicator addresses opportunities others pass by or that others aren't skilled enough to consider trying. That courageous, role model communicator can be YOU if you want it to be—a savvy risk-taker who adds value to each interaction. I try to keep in mind this encouragement and admonition from American author and activist Alice Walker: "The most common way people give up their power is by thinking they don't have any."

I've studied risk-taking communicators for many years and that's a big part of how I became one myself. Complete risk-taking communicators have some interesting commonalities. They've hunted for their hidden challenges, and faced their weaknesses with heart. They work to get good at speaking and writing so their messages are met with action. They are resilient. They unplug sometimes. They view time as the gift that it is and understand that life is short. They are inclusive and empathic. They feel their fears and act despite them.

These brave souls rarely expend energy trying to prove themselves correct. They ask open-ended questions to learn about others. They prioritize then publicize their goals. Their values and thoughts align with their words and deeds. They're humble, crediting those upon whose shoulders they stand. They know who they're here to serve. They document their dreams and goals. They are much more likely to reach their potential as communicators compared to those who bypass risk. If they're naturally other-affirmed, they build self-affirmation. If self-affirmed, they try to place more emphasis on how others see them. They are on the lookout for hidden obstacles to growth (lies they might tell themselves, rationalizations, reverberations of past griefs). They empower themselves and others. They use their unique communication gifts to their full potential to benefit self and others, and that may be the biggest *Pro Move* of all.

When you end this day, will you be satisfied with how you communicated with those who share your world? Were you brave, willing to express yourself—or brave in a different and equally valuable way: willing to listen attentively? Were you in a hurry, or did you slow down long enough to convey that you care? Did you extricate yourself from an unproductive conversation to better use your time? *Pro Moves* all. As author Nancy Thayer said, "It's never too late in fiction or life to revise." As long as you're living, you get another chance tomorrow. If you took a risk and it didn't go well, you can apologize or revise using what you've learned from the valuable mistakes you make today.

CHAPTER 10 Pro Move

Benchmark inspiring people who live their mission. Study how they communicate. This could be at your place of employment, doctor's office, car repair shop, favorite restaurant, in the world of sports, or just about anywhere. When these folks wow you, ask yourself, "Am I as engaged as they are?" and if necessary, "What am I missing?"

CHAPTER 10 Exercise

List—for your eyes only—some people in your in-group and out-group. Choose a few from your out-group and move toward them sincerely, risking rejection with the goal to improve your relationship just a little. Four solid options include:

1. Ask an open-ended question, to encourage more than a yes/no answer: "What do you think about X?" "How is your project going?"

2. Make eye contact. Drop in briefly to get some face time.

3. Offer sincere praise and helpful feedback.

4. Share some information of possible interest to the other person, personally or professionally.

If the risk doesn't work out and you get a cold shoulder, you'll be OK. The discomfort you feel is learning mode at its finest. And if things go well, your risk may pay off with an improved relationship. What a win that would be, because it's our friends who make our world.

CONCLUSION

Be Steadfast in Your Courage

Life is a shipwreck, but we must not forget to sing in the lifeboats.

—VOLTAIRE, FRENCH WRITER
AND PHILOSOPHER

YOU'VE ARRIVED AT THE END of this book hopefully knowing you never "arrive" fully as a communicator. The waves will keep coming. You'll lose your footing and start again. Brave communication doesn't follow a step-by-step recipe, so don't let anyone tell you it does. There's no one right way to do it. You never graduate, but as you take smart risks, your communication becomes more powerful. This lands you some exciting opportunities you may not have believed you'd see—the kind that have you grinning as you call a friend to say, "You're not going to believe what happened!" An interesting side effect of success is finding yourself a beginner again, tested by new scenarios, needing to call upon your courage yet again. Courageous communication keeps opening new doors. It becomes *who you are* more than *what you do* when you welcome risk for a higher purpose in everyday interactions.

I watched a tai chi video and the instructor (Master Lam Kam-Chuen) offered something that tickled me. It's brilliant advice about holding one position with your body (or communication goal: courage) for what seems like a long time: "Don't bother to give up." Exactly right! As you stumble in your attempts at brave communication, don't bother to give up. Go forward determined to grow as someone who accepts setbacks, and your growth is a given in the long run.

We develop courage as we go. Whether you're 19 or 92, each time you try a *Pro Move*, you gain guts to face your next challenge. It's like building muscle. What you do next, and next after that is communication improvisation. It comes uniquely from you, adding something to the mix that we all lose if you don't push yourself a little. As you make up *Pro Moves* of your own, your heart, body, and mind work together. You become a medium through which communication is more effective and meaningful. It's the practice, not the perfect, that matters most.

I hope the time you've spent considering courageous *Pro Moves* creates many positive returns for you. I truly believe beautiful rewards await outside your comfort zone as you explore new ways to interact. Of course, it's not just your world you impact for the better, it's ours. As you seize opportunities to be brave, sometimes you get the joy of seeing a risk pay off, while other positive outcomes happen unseen. Still, every effort counts. We notice your communication. We notice your participation. We can be deeply influenced by your choices and your unique flair. You've got role model potential; that is a fact. There's a Dakota Sioux proverb: "*We will be known forever by the tracks we leave.*" Your courage helps you clarify what you stand for so you can speak, write, and listen in alignment with your values.

Your reputation and happiness are determined to a large extent by your communication. It is your autograph and your art. When your fear rises up, remember you are never alone in that emotion. We're all afraid sometimes. Acting despite your fear is the key to overcoming hidden challenges. Fear is a friend that reminds us we'll have to choose to continue despite it. The world is your communication canvas and your palette is always expanding. Now go and paint your masterpiece!

> *If you hear a voice inside you saying, "You are no painter,"* then **paint by all means** *and that voice will be silenced, but only by working.*

> —VINCENT VAN GOGH,
> DUTCH POST-IMPRESSIONIST PAINTER

NOTES

CHAPTER 1

Topor, David. "If You Are Happy and You Know It . . . You May Live Longer." *Harvard Health Blog,* 2019. https://www.health.harvard .edu/blog/if-you-are-happy-and-you-know-it-you-may-live-longer -2019101618020.

Fourteenth Dalai Lama, and Howard C. Cutler. *The Art of Happiness at Work.* New York: Riverhead Books, 2003, 30-31.

Merrill, David W., and Roger H. Reid. *Personal Styles & Effective Performance.* West Chester: Chilton Book Company, 1981.

CHAPTER 3

Wheeler, John Archibald. "The Outsider." *Newsweek,* March 1979.

Orcutt, Daniel. "Sure to Win." *The Shaker Manifesto,* vol 8, no. 1, January 1979, 224.

CHAPTER 4

Lupoli, Matthew, Lily Jampol, and Christopher Oveis. "Lying Because We Care: Compassion Increases Prosocial Lying," *Journal of Experimental Psychology: General*, 2017.

Schwartzberg, Joel. *Get to the Point!: Sharpen Your Message and Make Your Words Matter*. Oakland: Berrett-Koehler Publishers, 2017, 4.

CHAPTER 6

Palmer, Parker J. *Healing the Heart of Democracy: The Courage to Create a Politics Worthy of the Human Spirit*. Nashville: John Wiley & Sons, 2014.

CHAPTER 7

Yu, Alisa, Justin M. Berg, and Julian J. Zlatev. "Emotional Acknowledgment: How Verbalizing Others' Emotions Fosters Interpersonal Trust." *Organizational Behavior and Human Decision Processes*, vol. 164, 2021, 116-35

CHAPTER 8

Consortium for Research on Emotional Intelligence in Organizations. "Reuven Bar-On, Ph.D. Biography." https://www.eiconsortium.org/members/baron.htm.

Salovey, Peter, and John D. Mayer. "Emotional Intelligence." *Imagination, Cognition and Personality*, vol 9, 1990, 185–211. doi: https://dx.doi.org/10.2190/DUGG-P24E-52WK-6CDG.

Goleman, Daniel. *Emotional Intelligence*. New York: Bantam Publishing, 1996.

Leimbach, Michael. "Redefining Employee Satisfaction: Business Performance, Employee Fulfillment, and Leadership Practices." Wilson Learning Worldwide. http://global.wilsonlearning.com/resources/employee-satisfaction/.

Bradberry, Travis. "Why You Need Emotional Intelligence to Succeed." TalentSmartEQ. https://www.talentsmarteq.com/articles/Why-You-Need-Emotional-Intelligence-To-Succeed-389993854-p-1 .html/.

CHAPTER 10
Zenger, Jack, and Joseph Folkman. "The 3 Elements of Trust." *Harvard Business Review*, 2019. https://hbr.org/2019/02/the-3-elements-of-trust.

Quade, Kristine, and Renée M. Brown. 2008. *The Conscious Consultant: Mastering Change from the Inside Out*. New York: John Wiley & Sons, 2001.

CONCLUSION
Stand Still and Be Fit. "Zhan Zhuang Day 10." YouTube video, 10:57, October 20, 2009. https://www.youtube.com/watch?v=-mbeZF28gtw&t=4s.

GRATITUDE

IT'S HUMBLING TO TAKE STOCK of how much help was needed to bring this book to fruition. Heartfelt thanks to my coaching clients, training participants, and generous family and friends who offered advice or a listening ear as it took shape.

Extra-special thanks to:

Tim Jones: You were when the idea was born and buoyed the project as a trusted friend, colleague, and editor for several years. For the mountain of improvements you made, all the evening and weekend meetings, hopping on a plane to work in person on the manuscript, and your refusal to grow tired of reading the same pages so many times, I'm forever grateful. It's no exaggeration to say I couldn't have done it without you.

The team at Gladieux Consulting, who generously apply their diverse, impressive expertise to make everything we do better, including this book: Elizabeth Baum, Elyse Bultemeier,

Michele Hill, Kelsey Martin, Kristen Schenkel, Heather Shively, Jason Swisher, and Sara Yarian. Our work together will always be one of the highlights of my career.

The dedicated team at BK Publishers, especially Jeevan Sivasubramaniam for his expert, guiding hand and mentorship. You've made me a better writer and even more importantly, a better feedback-receiver. Neal Maillet: your keen eye, creative suggestions, and sense of humor helped this book reach its potential. Anna Leinberger, thank you for your input as the book took shape. To Mike Crowley, thank you for sharing your marketing expertise. I thank the full team at BK, especially Katelyn Keating, Valerie Caldwell, Ashley Ingram, Shanzeh Khurram, Katie Sheehan, Courtney Schonfeld, Leslie Crandell, María Jesús Aguiló, and Catherine Lengronne. This book is better because of you.

For his assistance with book design and production and patience with final edits, I thank Richard Whitaker at Seventeenth Street Studios. I appreciate the collaboration on cover art from Susan Malikowski of DesignLeaf Studio. For excellence in copy editing, I thank Todd Manza. I'd also like to thank Matthew White for indexing and David Sweet for proofreading. Penguin Random House team: I appreciate all the behind-the-scenes work you contributed to this project.

Three gifted professional writers made time to review the manuscript and elevate its style and content. I was lucky to have input from these savvy authors: Jackie Stavros, Jill Swenson, and Aspen Baker.

For sharing a generous amount of time, creativity, enthusiasm, and suggestions to improve this book's voice and form:

Mark Gladieux

Dr. Karl Einolf

Dr. Jill Ihsanullah
Dr. Jon Walker
Surge Sen
Dave Kaverman
Stephen Best
Sheena Weller
Emily Blackman
Mike Amundson
Dawn Black
Christine Boles
Matt Mullin
James Chao
Jean and Brian Groat
Jeneatte Rude
Dean Soll
Andrew Booth
Rick Doering
Shane Armstrong
Gordon Groat
Paul Hanna
Linda Young
Robert Herzog
Jill Bartosh
Dr. Scott Smith
Jennifer Hill-Phillips
Ann Waters
Mike Cahill

For courageously sharing their communication struggles and wins with me: my college students at Purdue University, Trine University, and Indiana Tech.

The folks above have rooted for me in many ways; they bless my life. To Dan Smyth and Rosemary Gladieux, I'm grateful for the stability and challenge you've brought to my life. May this book earn the honor of its dedication to you by improving the lives of those who read it.

INDEX

ABOUT THE AUTHOR

MICHELLE GLADIEUX is an executive coach, instructional designer, teacher, and keynote speaker deeply committed to helping people overcome fears about communication to spark professional and personal growth. She earned her M.S. degree at Purdue University in West Lafayette, Indiana, and has designed and presented over one thousand original  seminars. She coaches clients to become more successful leaders and communicators in corporate, nonprofit, academic, government, and military settings. When it's downtime, you'll find her at one of her favorite places on Earth: a lake in Indiana, a beach on the Gulf Coast, or at a live music show. Michelle's nickname since 6th grade is "Glad," and she strives daily to live up to it with a grateful heart.

⊛ Berrett–Koehler
B̄K̄ Publishers

Berrett-Koehler is an independent publisher dedicated to an ambitious mission: *Connecting people and ideas to create a world that works for all.*

Our publications span many formats, including print, digital, audio, and video. We also offer online resources, training, and gatherings. And we will continue expanding our products and services to advance our mission.

We believe that the solutions to the world's problems will come from all of us, working at all levels: in our society, in our organizations, and in our own lives. Our publications and resources offer pathways to creating a more just, equitable, and sustainable society. They help people make their organizations more humane, democratic, diverse, and effective (and we don't think there's any contradiction there). And they guide people in creating positive change in their own lives and aligning their personal practices with their aspirations for a better world.

And we strive to practice what we preach through what we call "The BK Way." At the core of this approach is *stewardship,* a deep sense of responsibility to administer the company for the benefit of all of our stakeholder groups, including authors, customers, employees, investors, service providers, sales partners, and the communities and environment around us. Everything we do is built around stewardship and our other core values of *quality, partnership, inclusion,* and *sustainability.*

This is why Berrett-Koehler is the first book publishing company to be both a B Corporation (a rigorous certification) and a benefit corporation (a for-profit legal status), which together require us to adhere to the highest standards for corporate, social, and environmental performance. And it is why we have instituted many pioneering practices (which you can learn about at www.bkconnection.com), including the Berrett-Koehler Constitution, the Bill of Rights and Responsibilities for BK Authors, and our unique Author Days.

We are grateful to our readers, authors, and other friends who are supporting our mission. We ask you to share with us examples of how BK publications and resources are making a difference in your lives, organizations, and communities at www.bkconnection.com/impact.

Dear reader,

Thank you for picking up this book and welcome to the worldwide BK community! You're joining a special group of people who have come together to create positive change in their lives, organizations, and communities.

What's BK all about?

Our mission is to connect people and ideas to create a world that works for all.

Why? Our communities, organizations, and lives get bogged down by old paradigms of self-interest, exclusion, hierarchy, and privilege. But we believe that can change. That's why we seek the leading experts on these challenges—and share their actionable ideas with you.

A welcome gift

To help you get started, we'd like to offer you a **free copy** of one of our bestselling ebooks:

www.bkconnection.com/welcome

When you claim your **free ebook**, you'll also be subscribed to our blog.

Our freshest insights

Access the best new tools and ideas for leaders at all levels on our blog at ideas.bkconnection.com.

Sincerely,

Your friends at Berrett-Koehler

Certified

Corporation